FOUR TIPPERARY SAINTS

Four Tipperary Saints

THE LIVES OF

Colum of Terryglass, Crónán of Roscrea
Mochaomhóg of Leigh

AND

Ruadhán of Lorrha

PÁDRAIG Ó RIAIN

FOUR COURTS PRESS

Typeset in 11.5 pt on 14 pt Garamond by
Carrigboy Typesetting Services for
FOUR COURTS PRESS LTD
7 Malpas Street, Dublin 8, Ireland
www.fourcourtspress.ie
and in North America for
FOUR COURTS PRESS
c/o ISBS, 920 NE 58th Avenue, Suite 300, Portland, OR 97213.

© Pádraig Ó Riain and Four Courts Press 2014

A catalogue record for this title is available
from the British Library.

ISBN 978-1-84682-550-7

Printed in England
by TJ International, Padstow, Cornwall.

Contents

Illustrations

Abbreviations

AClon.	Annals of Clonmacnoise being the Annals of Ireland from the earliest period to AD 1408, ed. D. Murphy (Dublin, 1896)
Acta sanctorum	*Acta sanctorum quotquot toto orbe coluntur*, ed. J. Bolland et al. (Antwerp and Brussels, 1643–)
add.	additional
ADFC	'Aided Diarmada meic Fergusa cerrbeoil' in S.H. O'Grady (ed.), *Silva gadelica (i–xxxi)*, 2 vols (London, 1892), i, 72–82
AFM	*Annála ríoghachta Éireann: Annals of the kingdom of Ireland by the Four Masters*, 7 vols, ed. J. O'Donovan (Dublin, 1848–51; 2nd ed. 1856; facs. repr. with intr. and appendix by K.N. Nicholls, Dublin, 1990)
AI	*The Annals of Inisfallen (MS Rawlinson B503)*, ed. S. Mac Airt (Dublin, 1951)
ATig.	'The Annals of Tigernach', ed. W. Stokes, in *Revue Celtique*, 16 (1895), 374–419; 17 (1896), 6–33, 119–263, 337–420; 18 (1897), 9–59, 150–97, 267–303; repr. 2 vols (Felinfach, 1993)
ATigIndex	*The Annals of Tigernach: index of names*, D. Ó Murchadha (London, 1997)
AU	*Annála Uladh: Annals of Ulster*, 4 vols, ed. W.M. Hennessy and B. Mac Carthy (Dublin, 1887–1901; facs. repr. with new intr. by N. Ó Muraíle, Dublin, 1998)
b.	barony
bb	baronies
BB	*The Book of Ballymote*, photo-lithogr. facs., with intr. by R. Atkinson (Dublin, 1887)
BNÉ	*Bethada náem nÉrenn. Lives of Irish saints*, 2 vols, ed. C. Plummer (Oxford, 1922)
Br	Brussels, Bibliothèque Royale MS 2324–40
Co.	County
col.	column
DIS	*A dictionary of Irish saints*, P. Ó Riain (Dublin, 2011)
E.	east(ern)
ed.	editor/edition
facs.	facsimile

Fiants	*The Irish fiants of the Tudor sovereigns (1543–1603)*, 4 vols (Dublin, 1879–90; repr. Dublin, 1994)
gen.	genitive
intr.	introduced by/introduction
LL	*The Book of Leinster, formerly Lebar na Núachongbála*, 6 vols, ed. R.I. Best, O. Bergin, M.A. O'Brien and A. O'Sullivan (Dublin, 1954–83)
Lr	Lower
M	Marsh's Library, Dublin, MS Z.3.1.5
MartG	*Félire hÚi Gormáin: The martyrology of Gorman*, ed. W. Stokes (London, 1895)
MartO	*Féilire Oengusso céli Dé: The martyrology of Oengus the Culdee*, ed. W. Stokes (London, 1905; repr. Dublin, 1984)
MartO1	'On the calendar of Oengus', ed. W. Stokes, *Transactions of the Royal Irish Academy*, 1 (1880), 1–32, i–ccclii
MartT	*The martyrology of Tallaght*, ed. R.I. Best and H.J. Lawlor (London, 1931)
MS	manuscript
MT	'The Monastery of Tallaght', ed. E.J. Gwynn and W.J. Purton, *Proceedings of the Royal Irish Academy*, 29C (1911), 115–79
N.	north(ern)
nr	near
OSLOY	*Ordnance Survey letters, Offaly*, ed. M. Herity (Dublin, 2008)
OSLTY	*Letters containing information relative to the antiquities of the county of Tipperary ... in 1840*, ed. M. O'Flanagan (Bray, 1930)
p.	parish
PHA	Petworth House Archive
repr.	reprint/reprinted
rev.	revised
R	Bodleian Library, Oxford, MS Rawlinson B485
RIA	Royal Irish Academy
S	Bibliothèque Royale, Brussels, MS 7672–4 (*Salmanticensis*)
S.	south(ern)
s.a.	*sub anno*
SAB	'Stair ar Aed baclámh' in S.H. O'Grady (ed.), *Silva gadelica (i–xxxi)*, 2 vols (London, 1892), i, 66–72
St	Saint

St.	Royal Irish Academy, Dublin, MS A iv 1
T	Trinity College Dublin, MS E.iii.11
TCD	Trinity College Dublin
terr.	territory/territorial
tl.	townland
tn	town
Upr	Upper
v.l.	*varia lectio*
VSHH	*Vitae sanctorum Hiberniae e Codice olim Salmanticensi*, ed. W.W. Heist (Brussels, 1965)
VSHP	*Vitae sanctorum Hiberniae*, 2 vols, ed. C. Plummer (Oxford, 1910; repr. 1968)
W.	west(ern)

COUNTIES

AH	Armagh	LH	Louth
AM	Antrim	LK	Limerick
CE	Clare	LM	Leitrim
CK	Cork	LS	Laois
CN	Cavan	MH	Meath
CW	Carlow	MN	Monaghan
DB	Dublin	MO	Mayo
DL	Donegal	OY	Offaly
DN	Down	RN	Roscommon
DY	Derry	SO	Sligo
FH	Fermanagh	TE	Tyrone
GY	Galway	TY	Tipperary
KE	Kildare	WD	Waterford
KK	Kilkenny	WH	Westmeath
KY	Kerry	WW	Wicklow
LD	Longford	WX	Wexford

Preface

LEAVING ASIDE EMLY, whose patron Ailbhe was Munster's principal saint, its 'second Patrick' with 'all Munster behind him', the patrons of four churches – Terryglass, Roscrea, Leigh and Lorrha – from within the present bounds of Co. Tipperary were made the subjects of Lives.[1] Of these, Lorrha and Roscrea became locations of priories of the canons regular of St Augustine in the course of the twelfth century, a development that, in my view, contributed to the production of the Lives of Crónán and Ruadhán.[2] Although there is no direct evidence to show that Terryglass attracted an external order, there are grounds for assuming that the Life of its patron Colum was also compiled by an Augustinian canon. The least notable of the four churches, Leigh, which, unlike the others, did not become the head of a parish, nonetheless attracted a biographer of its saint. This may have been because of the place it apparently occupied among the possessions of the Cistercian abbey of Kilcooly, founded by Domhnall Mór Ua Briain about 1182 and affiliated to Jerpoint Abbey a few years later.[3] Each of the four Lives presented here was originally written in Latin, and although two, those of Ruadhán and Mochaomhóg, were later translated – or adapted – into Irish, none has hitherto been fully translated into English.[4] As texts in Latin have become unintelligible to most modern readers, it is appropriate that access to the contents of these four Lives be now widened by the provision of translations into English.

The decision to begin work on this book was taken following a conversation with George Cunningham at one of this twice-yearly conferences on Medieval Ireland in Roscrea; quite rightly, he considered it lamentable that few are now in a position to read texts written in Latin. I am indebted to my colleague, Kevin Murray, for having read the work and for having suggested many improvements. I am also grateful to Diarmuid Ó Riain for help with some

---

1 For Ailbhe, see *DIS* 58–60.   2 Gwynn and Hadcock, *Medieval religious houses*, 185, 192.   3 Ibid., 137.
4 The Irish translations, of which only that of Ruadhán has been published, are in a form of the language no longer familiar to modern readers (*BNÉ* i, 317–29). Previous translations into English, accompanied by commentary, of extracts from the Lives by John O'Hanlon and John Gleeson are to be found in O'Hanlon, *The Lives*, iii, 338–61 (Mochaomhóg); iv, 148–66 (Ruadhán), 516–30 (Crónán), and in Gleeson, *History*, 233–44 (Ruadhán), 348–62 (Crónán), 423–31 (Colum), 566–79 (Mochaomhóg). Gleeson's translation of Mochaomhóg's Life, while lacking commentary, is almost complete. Several passages and chapters were passed over, however, sometimes on the apparent basis that their contents were unseemly.

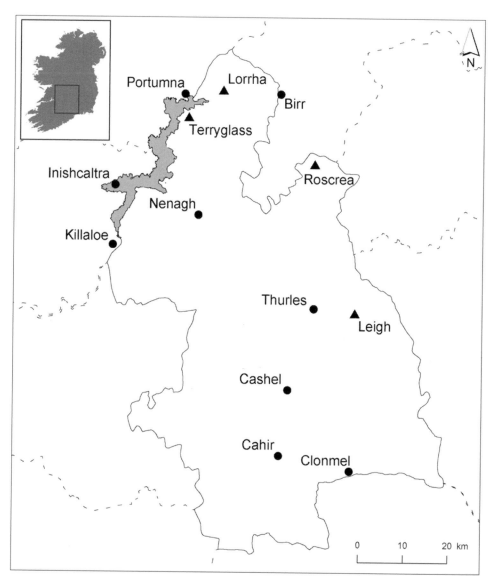

1 Map showing the locations of the four churches in Tipperary whose saints were made the subjects of written Lives (shown as triangles; other places shown as circles) (map prepared by Gary Devlin and the Discovery Programme).

cruxes in the Latin texts. Finally, thanks are due to Michael Potterton for the care with which he copy-edited the volume and, last but not least, to University College Cork and the National University of Ireland for their support.

Editorial policy

THE TRANSLATION OF THE TEXTS, though faithful, is not literal. Its purpose is to provide readable and easily comprehensible texts. Consequently, such usages in the Latin texts as the recurrent application of *sanctus*, 'holy', to the saint's name are often ignored here, as are the repetitive naming practices that are again characteristic of the Latin texts. Connectives (and, but, when, while, where etc.) are often either added or omitted, and demonstratives (this, that) are often replaced by the articles (a, the). Sometimes, when they add nothing to the sense of the words about them, such terms as 'however' (Latin *autem*) are also omitted. Latin words such as *locus* and *civitas* are frequently used in the original texts for churches, monastic sites or communities. Consequently, where the context allows, use is made in the translations of either 'church', 'monastery' or 'monastic town'. As a rule, place-names are rendered here by their anglicized forms but, where these are either unknown or no longer used, the Irish forms are retained. Similarly, territorial names are anglicized where appropriate, as in Ossory for Osraighe, but left unchanged where confusion might occur, as in Midhe, which denoted mainly Westmeath; Múscraighe Tíre, which denoted what are now the baronies of Ormond; and Éile, which comprised baronies in both Tipperary and Offaly. Personal names are, however, always given their classical Irish forms.

As none of the Lives can be discussed in isolation from the church associated with its subject, an account of the relevant church's documentary history, in as far as this can now be established, is given in the introduction to each translation. To avoid clutter in the translations, notes to the texts are added at the end of the volume. Finally, with a view to facilitating use of the volume, lists of abbreviations, sources and an index have been provided.

The Life of Colum of Terryglass

THE SAINT

O**F ALL FOUR TIPPERARY CHURCHES,** Terryglass (Irish *Tír Dá Ghlas*, 'land of two streams') has the longest documented history; it is already mentioned in the Life written for Colum Cille by Adhamhnán at the end of the seventh century.[1] Latinized by Adhamhnán as *Ager Duorum Rivorum* and *Rus Duum Rivulorum*, these forms were thought to refer to *Tír Dá Chraobh*, now Teernacreeve in the Westmeath parish of Castletown-Kindalen, but William Reeves set the record straight in a lengthy note added to his edition of Adhamhnán's text.[2] The text describes how Colum Cille arrived at Terryglass when the keys of the oratory had been lost. Approaching the door, the visitor from Iona proclaimed that God was capable of opening it without keys, following which the door duly sprang open. Entering the church ahead of all others, the saint was warmly received and revered with honour. The reverence shown to him in this passage has been taken to indicate that Colum Cille was the original patron of Terryglass, and that Colum son of Nainnidh (or Criomhthann) was a later localization of the Iona saint.[3]

How early Colum of Terryglass came to be regarded as a separate saint is now undiscoverable. The assertion that he fell victim to the 'great mortality' of 551, together with Finnian of Clonard, though partly at one with the narrative of the Life written for each of these saints, is retrospective and, consequently, unreliable.[4] Among others said to have succumbed to the plague is Colum of the island of Inishcaltra, a probable double of Colum of Terryglass, whose Life not only allows him to establish himself on the island, but also locates his remains on it for seven years (§§16–20, 30). Another indication of the unreliability of the list of those who succumbed to the plague is that the three churches named in the list – Inishcaltra, Killeigh and Kilcullen – are

---

1 Reeves, *The Life of St Columba*, 152 (2.37). 2 Ibid., 152–3n. 3 Ó Briain, 'The hagiography of Leinster', 462n; Ó Riain, 'Towards a methodology', 150–1. For a detailed discussion of the varying use of the patronymics in relation to Colum, see Sperber, 'One saint, two fathers'. Sperber suggests that use of Criomhthann reflects a Munster perspective whereas use of Nainnidh points to a Leinster bias. Coincidentally, Criomhthann was also the name originally given to Colum Cille (Ó Riain, *Corpus*, §§397, 661, 703.1.22). 4 Ó Riain, *The making of a saint*, 14–15.

Acta Sancti Columbae

de Tyre da Glass.

Incipit de Sancto Columba Tyre da Glass.

1. SANCTUS Columba de genere nobili Lagenensium de gente Chrauntanani ortus fuit.Cujus pater, nomine Naindith, rex fuit potens ; mater vero ipsius vocabatur Minchlu. Hoc autem mirabile in ejus conceptione factum est [1]. Nam ex die qua

3. ALIO quoque die duo angeli in formis avium, scilicet cignorum, apparuerunt supra domum [3] in qua infans positus erat, et nimio ardore et splendore illam domum repleverunt ; et vox eorum et ale [4] illorum suavia cantabant carmina [5], ita ut homines audientes dormirent. Tunc unus angelus ad alterum dixit: *Unus ex nobis ad custodiendum puerum maneat, et alter pergat ut* [6] *ad bapti-*

2 Title and opening passage of the Life of Colum of Terryglass, published from the Salamancan codex in De Smedt and Backer, *Acta sanctorum Hiberniae*, cols 445–6.

otherwise first recorded by the annals in the mid- to late eighth century.[5] Also, the Uí Chriomhthannáin, the family to which Colum was attached by the genealogists, appear to have first gained control of the abbacy of Terryglass shortly before the middle of the ninth century; Aodh son of Dubh Dá Chríoch, the first abbot of the family to be noticed by the annalists, died in 845 (*AU*).

The Uí Chriomhthannáin (or Uí Chriomhthainn Áin) were a Leinster family that held lands near Stradbally on Laois's border with Kildare, and earlier also in the area about Portlaoise. Colum's mother Mionchloth, a name also borne by Colum Cille's sister, is said to have been a sister of Caoimheall, mother of Caoimhghin of Glendalough, whose people were the Dál gCormaic Loisc (otherwise the Uí Chormaic) of the area between Killeshin in Carlow and Killabban in Laois.[6]

Described as a 'descendant of a true prince', Colum, who was likened in manners to the apostle and evangelist Matthew, came to be regarded as one of the twelve apostles of Ireland.[7] His connection with Terryglass, although

5 *AU* 746, 785. 6 Ó Riain, *Corpus*, §722.20; Reeves, *The Life of St Columba*, 247 (Colum Cille's sister Mionchloth was reputedly the mother of the sons of Éanán, patrons of Kilmacrenan); Bhreathnach, 'The

regular in the non-biographical record, is devoid of emphasis in the saint's Life. According to this (§19), he only glimpsed Terryglass while in passage on Lough Derg, spending most of his time instead either on Inishcaltra or on an island in the Shannon Estuary. He was summoned from the latter island to minister at the deathbed of Finnian of Clonard in Co. Meath, before himself dying on the following day in the neighbouring church of Clonee. His remains, it is said, took many years to arrive in Terryglass.[8]

THE CHURCH

As already stated, Terryglass's record begins with its mention in the Life written by Adhamhnán (d. 704) for his predecessor on Iona. It is the only Munster church mentioned by name and its presence in the text suggests that it then formed part of Iona's widely flung *parochia* or federation of churches.[9] This inference is supported by the lack of any reference to Terryglass in the seventh-century Lives compiled for Patrick of Armagh and Brighid of Kildare whose *parochiae* then rivalled that of Iona in extent. Neither Muirchú, Tíreachán nor Cogitosus, the authors of these Lives, brings his subject to this part of the province of Munster. Furthermore, when a new Life in three parts was compiled for Patrick in the middle of the ninth century, Terryglass was again ignored, despite the itinerary mapped out for the saint, which brought him to Múscraighe Tíre, the territory containing Colum's church. Perhaps significantly, this was also about the time that the Uí Chriomhthannáin of Leinster first appear to have taken over the abbacy of Terryglass.[10] In addition to their provision of successors to Colum at Terryglass, the Uí Chriomhthannáin also provided abbots of Clonenagh in Co. Laois, whose patron, Fiontan, belonged to the same family as Brighid of Kildare.[11] It could be, therefore, that by the middle of the ninth century, when an Uí Chriomhthannáin presence is first attested in Terryglass, the church had become affiliated either to Clonenagh or to the much greater *parochia* of Kildare. In this regard, it is worth noting that Colum is said to have been reared at Clonkeen in the parish of Clonenagh

genealogies of Leinster', 260.   7 O'Brien, *Corpus*, 122b26; Ó Riain, *Corpus*, §712.10; Grosjean, 'Les vies de S. Columba', 346–7; *VSHH* 83 §5.   8 My reference in *DIS* (p. 210) to Colum's 'finally settling in Terryglass' is inaccurate.   9 As I speculatively suggested in Ó Riain, *The making of a saint*, 16, on the basis of a reference to Clonard's *parochia* in Munster in *AU* 787, Terryglass may by then have been affiliated to it. Cf. Sperber, 'One saint, two fathers', 192.   10 It has been argued that Glendalough may have had a prior interest in Terryglass, but, as pointed out by Sperber ('One saint, two fathers', 174–5), the evidence for this is as confusing as it is slight (Mac Shamhráin, *Church and polity*, 210).   11 Ó Riain, *Corpus*, §3;

3 The Church of Ireland church in Terryglass is attached to two earlier walls of a large church with trabeate west door. Despite Colum's patronage of the church, it was only after his death that his remains were brought here (image courtesy of Colum Hardy).

by another member of the Uí Chriomhthannáin family (§4).[12] Furthermore, Fiontan figures prominently in the text of Colum's Life, which gives an account of how and why he chose Clonenagh (§§13–14).

A very full list of abbots of Terryglass, extending from Nadh Caoimhe, alias Mochaoimhe (d. 584), Colum's companion (§§14, 17, 19, 28–31), to Aodh Mac Criomthainn, compiler of the so-called Book of Leinster, who appears to have lived until the early years of the thirteenth century, has been preserved.[13] Aodh's family, as already stated, appears to have first gained control of the abbacy in the early ninth century, about the time that an outstanding representative of the *céili Dé* – a group within the Irish Church that thought of themselves as 'clients of God' – was nearing the end of his life in Terryglass. This was Maol Díthreibh, the notice of whose death in 840 (*AFM*) describes him as *angcoire agus eagnaidh* (anchorite and wise man). Maol Díthreibh is

O'Brien, *Corpus*, 126a28–31.   **12** Cf. Sperber, 'One saint, two fathers', 182.   **13** Gwynn and Gleeson, *A history*, 38–47; *LL* i, xvi–xvii. For Nadh Caoimhe, see *DIS* 459. Sperber ('One saint, two fathers', 186–9) argues that gaps in the reporting of obits in the Annals of Inisfallen and Annals of Ulster may

best known for his role in the preservation of the teachings of Maol Ruain, which appear to have been written down by a cleric personally acquainted with the Tallaght saint.[14] In addition to a series of questions put by Maol Díthreibh to Maol Ruain – which provide crucial evidence of the rule followed in Tallaght – he is credited with a question put to another prominent associate of the *céili Dé*, Ealáir of Loch Cré (Monaincha), who died in 807.[15] Possibly provided with a substantial pre-Romanesque church in the eleventh century, which was burned three times in the course of the twelfth century – in 1112, 1140 and 1164 – Terryglass subsequently received no mention in the Irish annals.[16]

THE LIFE

According to his Life (§3), Colum, having been baptized by Momhaodhóg of Fiddown, was reared at Clonkeen in the parish of Clonenagh by Colmán Cúile; both Momhaodhóg and Colmán also belonged to the Uí Chriomhthannáin.[17] He then attended the famous school of Finnian at Clonard, with, among others, Colum Cille, before going first to Rome, where he received relics of Peter and Paul, and then to Tours in France, which he left, after some miracles, with enshrined relics of St Martin (§§7–9). His attendance at Finnian's school, and his concern with obtaining relics of Peter and Paul allow for the possibility that the author of the Life was a canon regular of St Augustine. Clonard was one of the more important early foundations of the canons in Ireland and, though it was dedicated to Mary, several priories of canons, including that at Armagh, were dedicated to the apostles.

On the way back to Ireland, Colum visited the part of Britain in which the Saxons lived, restoring to life there children of the king and converting the people to belief in Christ (§§10–11). As in the Life of Abán of Adamstown, where similar claims are made, this visit probably reflects the need felt by Irish clerics to take issue with the contention of twelfth-century English churchmen that the Irish Church was in great need of reform.[18]

Arriving back in Ireland, Colum was first brought to his native place among the Uí Chriomhthannáin where, on a site granted by his brother Cairbre, he founded a church known as Eadarghabhal, before eventually leaving in it a

reflect differing claims as to whether Colum of Terryglass was of Munster or Leinster origin. **14** Gwynn and Gleeson, *A history*, 40–2; Follet, *Céli Dé in Ireland*, 2, 90–1, 101. **15** Gwynn, 'The Rule of Tallaght', 21; Follet, *Céli Dé in Ireland*, 90–2. **16** *AFM* 1112, 1164; ATig. 1140; Ó Carragáin, 'Patterns of patronage', 30–1. **17** Ó Riain, *Corpus*, §242.1. **18** A similar approach is adopted in the Life of Abán

disciple named Crónán. Though Eadarghabhal has remained unidentified, it must have lain in or near lands either owned by or associated with the Uí Chriomhthannáin. These were located approximately in eastern Laois, in a triangle formed by Clonenagh, Timahoe and Stradbally, an area which, to my knowledge, contained no place called Eadarghabhal (later Addergoole or something similar).[19] There is, however, a place called Addergoole about fifteen miles south-west of Timahoe in the parish of Aghmacart, later the site of a nunnery belonging to the Augustinian canonesses at Kilculliheen.[20] Between this and Timahoe, in the parish of Dysartgallen, is Kilcronan, a name that may recall Colum's disciple. Furthermore, both Clonenagh and Anatrim, whose patrons (Fiontan and Caomhán) are introduced in the following section (§13), were located within ten miles or so of Addergoole and would have lain on the way northwards to Cloney in the Kildare parish of Kilberry, which Colum and his companions were encouraged to leave (§13). But even if Addergoole were to be the place intended, the question would remain as to why Fiontan and Caomhán joined up with Colum before the journey to Cloney, rather than after it when Clonenagh was visited.

Subsequent to his stay in Clonenagh, Colum and his companions went westwards to the territory of Uí Mhaine, later the equivalent of the diocese of Clonfert, where the saint founded a church at a place named Tír Snámha (§15).[21] This place has yet to be identified, but it may have lain in the area about Snámh Dá Éan, a crossing place of the River Shannon at Cloonburren in the Roscommon parish of Moore, opposite Clonmacnoise. The saint then allegedly founded several churches in the area about Lough Derg, before arriving at Inishcaltra (alias Holy Island), where his stay is spread over several sections (§§15–19). As his remains were also later buried there for a period of seven years (§30), we may take it that the dedicatees of the island, Caimín (a pet form of Colum) and a supposedly distinct other Colum, were in fact doubles of the saint.[22] His stay at Inishcaltra provided an opportunity of seeing Terryglass from a distance and expressing the wish that his remains would one day be buried there (§19). At no point in the Life is it said that he either founded the church or stayed on the site. Instead, he was brought by his biographer to an island called 'Insula Erce', later 'Inisherke', or 'Enish Sherkey', near Canon Island, the site of an Augustinian priory in the Fergus Estuary of

---

(*VSHH* i, 10–12 §§13–14; Ó Riain, 'St Abbán', 165).   **19** Ó Murchadha, 'Early history', 51.   **20** Carrigan, *The history and antiquities*, ii, 234–5; iv, 205. Cf. Sperber, 'One saint, two fathers', 190.   **21** For some possible implications of the Uí Mhaine episode, see Sperber, 'One saint, two fathers', 181.   **22** For Caimín, see *DIS* 136–7, 210. Colum of Inishcaltra is said to have died, with Colum of Terryglass, of the 'great

the River Shannon (§20).[23] Here, an angel informed him of 'three orders of men' who would gain heaven only through his merits, between 'Inisherke' and Inishcaltra, Inishcaltra and Clonenagh, Clonenagh and Agha, the latter a church in Co. Carlow. No explanation is provided for the choice of these places, one of which, Agha, is otherwise left without mention in the Life. A connecting thread is supplied, however, by the Life of Fiontan of Clonenagh, which, in one episode, allows its subject to be visited at Agha by a bishop named Brannabh.[24] Lying within the territory of the Uí Dhróna, now Idrone barony, Agha is not far from Lorum, a church associated with Colum of Terryglass.[25] The suspicion must be, therefore, that the ecclesiastical family of Uí Chríomhthannáin, which is known to have provided abbots at Clonenagh and Terryglass, also had hereditary interests at Agha.

While on the island, the saint was visited by Neasán of Mungret who requested that Colum mediate between him and heaven (§24). Since Mungret is thought to have been affiliated to the canons regular, this may be another indication of Augustinian influence on the Life.[26] Although lacking any early documentary support, an affiliation of this kind would be in keeping with the Augustinian practice of placing their foundations at or near diocesan cathedrals. Mungret was the chief early church of the territory of Uí Fhidhgheinte, later approximately the area covered by the diocese of Limerick, and, until passed over in favour of the church of St Mary within the town of Limerick as the cathedral church of the diocese, it would have enjoyed a very high status.[27] Later, the church and its lands were granted by Domhnall Ua Briain to the church of St Mary.[28]

The remainder of the text is devoted to Colum's time on the island of 'Inisherke', from which he was summoned to Clonard to attend Finnian on his deathbed (§26). Finnian is said to have foretold that Colum would administer the last rites to him and, having duly done so, Colum proceeded to Clonee in the Meath parish of Trim, some five miles from Clonard, where he died on the following day (§27). This sequence of events reflects the arrangement of the martyrologies, which place the feasts of the two saints on successive days, 12/13 December.[29] The remains of the saint were first laid to rest in Clonee for either one or seven years before being taken, despite great opposition from the Uí Néill, to Terryglass. En route, the remains first reached

mortality' in 549 (*AU*). **23** Gwynn and Hadcock, *Medieval religious houses*, 162. See note to §20 at pp 89–90, below. **24** *VSHP* ii, 104 §19. **25** Ó Riain, *Corpus*, §§667–8. **26** Gwynn and Hadcock, *Medieval religious houses*, 199. **27** Ibid., 90. **28** Flanagan, *Irish royal charters*, 317–18 (no. 7). **29** *MartO* 251; *MartG* 236–8.

Clonmacnoise, where Abbot Aonghas sought to retain the body, and then
Inishcaltra, where it lay buried for another seven years (§§29–30);
Clonmacnoise also hosted a priory of canons regular.[30]

In sum, although sometimes thought to be an early composition, in its
choice of places visited by Colum, or otherwise associated with him, the saint's
Life reflects circumstances unlikely to have obtained until after the arrival in
Ireland of the canons regular of St Augustine in the early twelfth century. Also,
the extensive ecclesiastical interests of the Uí Chriomhthannáin family appear
to have influenced the choice of saints featured in the Life as well as the itinerary
followed by the saint from his home place in east Laois to an island called
'Inisherke' in the Fergus Estuary of the River Shannon.

In her discussion of the Life, Ingrid Sperber, while admitting the possibility
of a final twelfth-century date, identifies three stages in the history of its
composition: an 'original Life', a stage at which Clonenagh episodes were
added, and a final Uí Chriomhthannáin-inspired stage.[31] The different
emphases in the Life are, indeed, worthy of note. In my view, however, all parts
of the text can be explained by reference to a single author, probably an
Augustinian canon, concerned with accommodating what appear to have been
complementary interests, some relating to his own order, others reflecting the
affairs of the Uí Chriomhthannáin.

MANUSCRIPTS AND PREVIOUS EDITIONS

Colum's Life survives in three manuscripts, in the so-called Salamancan codex
in the Bibliothèque Royale in Brussels, shelf number 7672–4, and in two
Rawlinson manuscripts, B 485 and B 505, one a copy of the other, in the
Bodleian Library, Oxford.[32] The Salamancan version has been twice edited
and published, first by C. De Smedt and J. De Backer in *Acta sanctorum
Hiberniae*, cols 445–62, then by W.W. Heist in *VSHH* 225–33. The Rawlinson
version, which is close to the Salamancan text, has yet to be edited. As Paul
Grosjean showed, an extract from Colum's Life, published by John Colgan in
his *Acta sanctorum*, 356–7, draws on both Rawlinson and Salamancan versions
of the Life.[33] Colgan appears also to have had at his disposal a Donegal codex,
now lost, to which he refers in a marginal note.[34] The present translation is
based on the Salamancan version, collated with the Rawlinson text.

---

30 Gwynn and Hadcock, *Medieval religious houses*, 165.   31 Sperber, 'One saint, two fathers', 196–8.
32 Plummer, *Miscellanea*, 241.   33 Grosjean, 'La vie de S. Columba'.   34 Ibid.

The Life of Colum of Terryglass

The beginning of [the Life]

1 ~ Colum of Terryglass belonged to the noble race of Criomhthannán (Uí Chriomhthannáin), a branch of the Leinstermen. His father Nainnidh was a powerful king and his mother was called Mionchlú. This is what happened by way of wonder at his conception: from the day of his conception in the womb until the day on which he was born his mother could neither eat meat nor drink wine, nor any other drink that might inebriate. This was because inebriation of the spirit from the grace of a holy son excluded intoxication of the body for the mother.

2 ~ On the night of the birth of the holy child, the house in which he was born was seen to glow in flames, at which all the inhabitants of the region came running in order to extinguish the fire. But when they came closer, they found the house safe, with no appearance of fire, and they saw an infant lying in the house in a brightness greater than the glittering light of the sun. Marvelling, they said: 'This infant will be great in heaven and on earth'.

3 ~ On another day, two angels appeared in the form of birds, that is to say swans, above the house in which the infant was lying, and they filled the habitation with great heat and brightness. The voices and wings of the birds rendered songs so sweet that the listening humans fell asleep. One angel then said to the other: 'Let one of us stay to watch over the boy, and let the other go and seek a priest to baptize him'. Immediately, one angel flew away and went to a holy man named Momhaodhóg of Fiddown who, rising up immediately and taking with him seven other bishops, came and baptized the boy with much respect.

4 ~ After this, the boy was brought to a certain holy man by the name of Colmán Cúile, founder of the church called Clonkeen. He then studied psalms and hymns with Colmán, who also reared him. When the boy Colum had grown

to become a young man, he went to Bishop Finnian at Clonard, studied with him, and was one of that holy school.

5 ~ It was customary in the holy school that, on his day, one or other of twelve [disciples] looked after the daily food of all the brethren, from wherever he might find it, be it by work or by purchase or by demanding it from others. On their days, the two Colums – namely Colum Cille and Colum son of Criomhthann – used to do this quietly without anxiety or preparation, and a dinner used to be found prepared by the Lord for the brethren. At this, the other holy men began to murmur as to why the privilege was given to these two by the Lord. Finnian responded: 'O my brethren, do not murmur about these, for they are two sons of kings who left behind an earthly kingdom and bodily sustenance, and this is why the privilege is granted to them by the Lord, because, if they were worldly, they would deserve to receive a meal daily'.

6 ~ Another night in that school, when Colum son of Criomhthann was alone in his little cell, reading by the light of lamps, these went out before the usual time and there was no oil in the house with which to moisten them. When Colum raised his right hand, however, his fingers shone like lamps. At that hour, one of his disciples came secretly from another house to see what Colum was doing in his little cell and, on looking in from outside, saw him reading from an open book, with the five fingers of his hand shining brightly above the book. This marvellous thing was seen on more than one night.

7 ~ When Colum had been instructed in every spiritual doctrine, he wished to go to Rome so that he might bring back from there relics of Peter and Paul. This pleased his master, who said to him: 'Go in peace and you will have a prosperous journey; you are leaving in good health and you will return in good health'. Finnian then grasped Colum's hand and said: 'O wonderful, cleansed hand, this most holy hand will give me the sacrament on the day of my death'. Colum accordingly went to Rome with his companions and brought back from there the relics of Peter and Paul, and he also came to the city of Martin to ask a favour of the Lord there, near the saint's relics. Martin had long since foretold his arrival there, for when he was ill unto death, he said to his people: 'Behold, after my death a certain holy guest of not ignoble race will come to you from the island of Ireland with such and such a number of companions in such and such clothing, and this guest will elevate my relics

from the grave at the appropriate time. Place, therefore, that chrismal and robe beside me in the shrine, because the guest will ask you for these insignia and you will give them to him'.

8 ~ When Colum came with his folk, therefore, to the town, they were immediately recognized, and the town was closed against them so that their virtue and faith might be tested. They fasted for three days and nights in front of the gates of the town and, during the three nights, the Lord made many miracles through them. On the first night, a great snow came down from heaven, but none at all fell where they were, and the snow made a circle at a distance around about them. On the second night, a strong wind blew so thunderously that it threw down many trees and houses, but did not stir even the hairs of their heads or the leaves of the books open in front of them; nor did it extinguish their lamps, which were lit. On the third night, a great rain fell but not a drop on the holy guests, and at last, having been allowed into the town, they proceeded to the church of Martin, where Colum elevated the relics of the blessed saint from the tomb and, washing them in water, placed them in a shrine decorated in gold and silver. Colum then received blessed Martin's robe and chrismal and took them with him.

9 ~ At that time, three men died in Martin's city, whereupon Colum, on being requested, went to the house in which the three corpses lay and, having invoked the name of Jesus Christ, raised the three to life.

10 ~ Having left that place behind, Colum proceeded to the part of Britain in which the Saxons were, up to then bound by pagan chains. Colum preached the word of God to them, and it so happened that in those days both son and daughter of their king died, and the bodies were brought to the grave with great mourning. The king then said to Colum: 'Three sons and three daughters of mine are buried in this place, and when you will have raised those six from the dead, I and all my people will believe in your Lord God'. At this, Colum prayed to God on bent knees and first brought back to life the king's son and daughter, whose corpses were lying in his presence. Then, turning again to the ashes, he prayed and raised from them to life the two sons and daughters who had previously died, and Colum said to them: 'Choose whether you will remain in this life with your parents or maintain the heavenly life'. They replied: 'Man of God, we choose and request that we go now without delay to the life in which we witnessed the just'. Thereupon, having been baptized, they went to

sleep again in the grave, on hearing of which the king and his people believed in Christ the Lord.

11 ~ In those regions, Colum performed many wonders but, in order to avoid human praise, he diligently concealed his miracles. One day, however, when Colum found some of his miracles written down in the book-chest of one of his disciples, he threw the book into the fire, burned it, and scolded his disciples with a severe rebuke. From that day on, therefore, none of his disciples dared to write down any of his miracles.

12 ~ After this, Colum returned to the lands of the Leinstermen on the island of Ireland in order to visit his own people. His brother Cairbre met him there and gave him a place called Eadarghabhal in which he left one of his disciples, a pilgrim named Crónán. This man said to Colum: 'If it pleases, father, I wish to be buried with you in one place and to rise from the dead with you in the same place'. Taking pity on the pilgrim, Colum said: 'Friend, let it be as you wish'. Stretching out his right hand, he detached his small finger without pain or wound and gave it to the disciple, saying: 'I and you will thus be buried together and, on the Day of Judgement, we shall rise together'. In the place, moreover, in which Colum's finger was pulled out, an evergreen hazel-tree sprang up, whose leaves, bark and shoots cure all feebleness and infirmity up to the present day.

13 ~ After this, with Colum's fame now spreading everywhere, three disciples joined up with him, namely Fiontan of the Maca Eachdhach, Caomhán of Anatrim and Mochaoimhe of Terryglass, and together they sought hither and thither a place in which to settle. On coming to a certain place in the lands of the Leinstermen, his companions said to Colum: 'It is good for us to be here'. But he said to them: 'This place has not been given by God to us, but to a certain, yet unborn, man'; this was Mobhí of the Maca Alla. From there they came to another place in which Clonenagh is now located, staying there for a year or longer, but leaving it when they could no longer put up with the gathering of men and friends.

14 ~ They then proceeded to the mountain of Smór, alias Slieve Bloom, where they found some boys guarding cattle, of whom the first, Séadna by name, was dumb from birth. Blessing his mouth, Colum said to him: 'Announce to us the places in which we shall rise from the dead'. Immediately the dumb

boy spoke and pointed out to each of them the exact place in which he would
settle and rise from the dead. Looking back from the mountain, Colum then
saw that the place from which they had come was being visited by angels, and
he became sad in that he had left it. His companions then said: 'O father,
what makes you sad?' He replied: 'If you were to see what I see, you would
rightly say that I do not become sad without reason, for I observe the place
from which we came to be full of angels, and between that same place and
heaven, angels do not cease from attending. Which one of us, therefore, will
set forth again for that place so that he may stay there forever?' Fiontan replied:
'Holy father, whichever one of us you say will set forth obediently'. Colum
said to him: 'Go in peace and God will be with you, young man, and stay in
that place until the day of your death'. After that, Fiontan came to the place
and stayed there. Nadh Caoimhe then said to his master: 'Behold, Fiontan
went off to his place, what shall I do. Shall I remain with you, as I greatly
desire, or will you set me up in another place?' Colum said: 'Look westwards
and observe there a lake stretching long and wide, because your community
will be on its shore, and you will be with me in the one place'.

15 ~ After these things, Colum went into the territory of the Connachta, where
he built a church at a place called Tír Snámha in the lands of the Uí Mhaine.
The number of his community there was 740, and he also held and spent
time in other places around Lough Derg, namely 'Aurraith Tophiloc' and
'Toim Boinden'. An angel of the Lord then appeared to him, to say: 'Arise
and go to Inishcaltra'. There he found an old man by the name of Mac Reithe,
to whom the angel said: 'Relinquish this island to Colum and go somewhere
else as a monk of his', which he did.

16 ~ Then, on the day of Colum's arrival on Inishcaltra, the Lord made a meal for
him, for there was a certain tree on the island by the name of lime-tree whose
sap, on dripping down, filled a vessel and had the taste of honey. The fluid
had the inebriating quality of wine, and Colum and his followers were sated
by this excellent liquid.

17 ~ Colum then lived on Inishcaltra for a long time, and the birds of the sky clung
intimately to him there, flying about his face and playing. At this, his disciple
Nadh Caoimhe said: 'Why, master, do the birds not take to flight from you;
they truly avoid us?' Colum replied: 'Why should birds avoid a bird? Just as
the bird flies, so does my mind never cease from flying to heaven'.

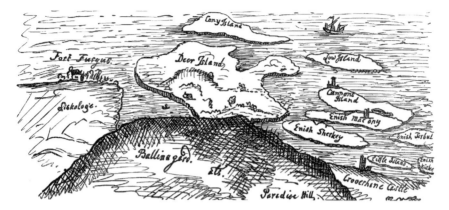

4 Drawing of islands at the confluence of the rivers Fergus and Shannon, made by Thomas Dineley in the journal of his Tour of Ireland in 1681, now National Library of Ireland MS 392 (from E.P. Shirley, Robert O'Brien and James Graves, 'Extracts from the journal of Thomas Dineley Esquire, giving some account of his visit to Ireland in the reign of Charles II', *Journal of the Kilkenny and Southeast of Ireland Archaeological Society*, 6 (1867), 85).

18 ~ On a certain day, when one of the brethren had been working outside the island, on its northern side, he died suddenly, and when this was announced to Colum, he said to the brethren: 'Go and say to him: Colum says to rise up in the name of Jesus Christ'. When the brethren had said this, he immediately rose from the dead as if from sleep and came safely to the island with them.

19 ~ On a certain other day, when Colum was sailing from Inishcaltra in Lough Derg with his disciples, Nadh Caoimhe and Fiontan of the Maca Eachdhach, he saw the place that is now Terryglass. Colum then rose up in the boat, sighed and said: 'Would that my resurrection were to be in that place'. This came to pass, for he was later buried in that place by his disciple Nadh Caoimhe.

20 ~ After these things, Colum, being unable to put up with the annoyance of the concourse of men and wishing to avoid human pomps, migrated from Inishcaltra to the Shannon Estuary. There he took possession of the Island of Earc, on which an angel of the Lord used to visit him frequently. On a certain day, when Colum and the angel were greeting one another, the latter said: 'Colum, you are beloved of the court of God on high'. Colum replied: 'It is customary for a father to grant the son whom he loves greatly a special gift beyond others; what gift of love shall I receive, therefore, from my God?' The angel said: 'Three orders of men who do not merit eternal life through

themselves will be given you by the Lord, and only through your merits, given freely and without good works, will they possess the kingdom of heaven. The first order stretches from this Island of Earc in the Shannon Estuary to Inishcaltra in Lough Derg; the second from Inishcaltra to the community of Clonenagh, the third from Clonenagh as far as the place called Agha'.

21 ~ On a certain other day, Colum went out to see the great water of the ocean and, as he walked hither and thither by the seashore, he suddenly stood still on a wide stone and said prophetically: 'In latter times my people will migrate from this stone with my relics to the Land of Promise in the sea'. That stone is called 'Colum's Stone' to this day.

22 ~ Another day, when Colum was walking about in the lands of the Tradraighe, he met a certain pregnant woman. On seeing her, he blessed her womb, saying: 'Blessed is this womb and the holy boy who lies in it, for he, together with others, will give me the sacrament on the day of my death'. This was Luchtighearn, who was later Colum's disciple and ministrant until the day of his master's death.

23 ~ On a certain other day on the Island of Earc, a most cunning wolf came and furtively stole and ate the lace of Colum's shoe. The wolf died immediately, and from that day on a wolf could neither live nor stay on the island because, if a wolf were to enter the island from outside by chance, it would die on that day or, just as dogs flee, it would immediately swim in terror from the island.

24 ~ On one of those days, the holy deacon Neasán went to Colum to request that he mediate between him and the Lord, as Patrick had foretold to him. For when deacon Neasán said to Patrick: 'Mediate between me and the Lord', Patrick replied: 'Another shepherd besides me who, coming from the East, will take possession of an island north-west of you, has been preordained for you by the Lord'. Ailbhe said the same to him, for when deacon Neasán had similarly requested of Ailbhe that he mediate between him and the Lord, he said: 'Another master has been ordained by God for you, namely Colum, who will later possess the Island of Earc in the Shannon Estuary'. When deacon Neasán then came to Colum, he accepted him.

25 ~ Colum used to go to another island near this Island of Earc to pray there regularly. On a certain day, when Colum wanted to go out to that island and

there was no boat ready, swans came to him and, with him sitting on their shoulders and with a most sweet song from their feathers, they carried him smoothly across the sea to the island. It was thus always; whenever Colum wished to make a journey between the two islands, the swans conveyed him quickly with their wings.

26 ~ When his master, Finnian of Clonard, saw the day of his death approaching, he requested of God that an angel come to him, in order to be sent by him to Colum, from whose hand, when he came, he might receive the body and blood of Christ. Finnian then wrote a letter to Colum to say that he should hasten without delay and, accepting the letter in his hand, the angel went off to Colum on the Island of Earc. Colum was most joyous at his arrival because of the honour [received] from angel and master, and because of his love of God, who sent the angel to him. Then Colum immediately arose and, as those who know say, he and his companions completed with the help of God in one day the ten-day journey between the Island of Earc in the Shannon Estuary and Clonard. Finnian was very happy at Colum's arrival and, on taking the sacrament from his hand, he died in the peace of Christ.

27 ~ When Colum had placed the body of his master in the grave with great honour, he went to a nearby place called Clonee, in which there was a pupil of his. Received there with great joy, Colum remained for the night, and at sunrise on the following day he ordered that a bath be prepared. On being asked by the brethren why he had ordered this, he said: 'Behold, the day of my death has arrived and a heavenly deputation came down to me, for the Lord is calling me to the heavenly feasts'. The brethren, sad and weeping copious tears, then made a bath and, when Colum had washed himself in it, he placed himself in a bed to sleep, while saying to his disciple Luchtighearn, who was nearby: 'My son, if you wish to die with me, wash yourself in the bath and come near me at the wall'. But he replied: 'Holy father, if it pleases you, I do not wish to die now because I did not procure, and I desire to make previous good works grow even more'. On hearing this, a certain rural layman, not yet baptized, who came to the door, said: 'O man of God, would that you had said to me to go with you to heaven'. Colum replied: 'If you believe in Christ with all your heart, receive the tonsure in our manner, wash your body and come next to me'. The countryman did all these things and placed himself next to Colum who, while comforting the brethren with spiritual words and bidding them farewell, went to sleep together with the countryman,

and went to heaven. At that hour, Colum Cille said to his brethren on the island of Iona: 'Brethren, pray because my colleague Colum has now performed a great miracle; he takes to heaven with him a pagan countryman without any work of penance, in the likeness of Christ and his thief'.

28 ~ Colum was buried there and reposed in the grave for seven years, as some say, or for one year, according to others. After that, his disciple Nadh Caoimhe, who wished to bring Colum's body to the community of Terryglass but feared that the Uí Néill might hold on to the body of the holy man, prudently made a plan. He filled twelve carts with grain and concealed a shrine containing the body of the holy man under the grain in the middle of one of them, for it was fitting that grain should be covered by grain. Nadh Caoimhe then led away the carts with his faithful companions, among whom was Odhrán, an honoured master concerning whom previously, when he was going into exile, the older Ciarán of Seirkieran had prophetically foretold, saying: 'O Odhrán, if you should go beyond the seas, you will come back again, and you will be through the provinces with Nadh Caoimhe in front of a cart full of grain containing Colum's body'. Having been divided up in this way, six of the carts journeyed through the lands of the Leinstermen on a long roundabout way, whereas the other six came with the holy treasure on a direct route through the lands of the Uí Néill to the community at Clonmacnoise.

29 ~ While they were there in the shelter for guests, this miracle took place; the shelter was seen to burn in flames of fire and the brethren, aroused from their beds, ran towards it in order to extinguish it, but, on arriving at the shelter, they saw no fire there, and again began to sleep in their beds. But what do I wait for? Three times that night the brethren were aroused to put out the fire. Aonghas, the abbot of the community, then questioned Nadh Caoimhe separately, saying: 'Tell me what you have with you on the journey in the way of something spiritual'. Nadh Caoimhe replied: 'Because you fear God, I shall reveal my secret to you; we have the body of my master hidden in the cart'. With hands outstretched and knees bent, Aonghas said: 'I give thanks to God who brought that treasure to us, for it will remain here with us forever'. Nadh Caoimhe then said: 'Do not do this, brother, for, when alive, he did not select this place for his resurrection. Let go, therefore, so that the anger of the heavenly God does not touch you, and I shall give you back a reward, because the name of your master Ciarán will precede the name of our master in the mass-book'. Aonghas then let them go.

30 ~ As morning came, they arrived at the River Shannon, where they found a
boat ready and prepared by the Lord, on entering which they began to sail.
Immediately, the Uí Néill, who were following them, filled the bank of the
River Shannon, and one of them, Colmán Beag, who was faster than the
others, took hold of the boat's rudder. Nadh Caoimhe said to him: 'Let us
go; otherwise you will soon die, and there will be no king of your race, and
you will press on into hell'. At this, he let them go, saying: 'Go in peace'. Sailing
from there, they came to Inishcaltra, where Colum's body reposed for seven
years and this marvellous thing then happened there; over the whole of Lough
Derg there was no darkness of night for three days and nights after the saint's
body was carried through it, and it is apparent from this that Colum has great
light in heaven.

31 ~ For seven years, as they relate, the Uí Néill laid siege to the community of
Terryglass, spying out as to when holy Colum's remains might be brought
back there. Despite all that, Nadh Caoimhe brought back the remains from
Inishcaltra on a certain night and, on their arrival, the whole place was seen
to light up like a bonfire, so that it became warm, and in all of Lough Derg,
through which the remains had been brought back, there was no darkness
for three days and nights. On witnessing these miracles, a certain holy man
of the encircling Uí Néill said to his friends: 'Let us desist from this business,
for this is the place selected by the saint so that his body might repose here
forever'. They then returned to their province, praising and blessing both the
Lord and Colum. On their departure, Colum's remains were placed with
great honour in a preordained spot, at which, through his merits, huge benefits
are granted daily by the Lord, through our Lord Jesus Christ, who has honour
and glory forever and ever.

The Life of Crónán of Roscrea

THE SAINT

CRÓNÁN SON OF ODHRÁN is said to have belonged to the Cianachta, among whose representatives were the Uí Chearbhaill (O'Carrolls) and Uí Mheachair (Mahers) of Éile, secular lords of the area about Roscrea.[1] According to one tradition, the saint's mother was Caoimhre, alias Mochaomhra, of the Corca Bhaiscinn of south-west Clare, whereas another source assigns the saint, with many unlikely siblings, including Ruadhán of Lorrha, to the offspring of Inghean Bhaoith of Killinaboy in Co. Clare.[2] Descent from Caoimhre provided Crónán with two notable cousins, both of whom were associated with the church of Lusmagh in Co. Offaly, a site which figures prominently in Crónán's Life (§§7–16). One, Mochonna, was a later patron of Lusmagh; the other, Baodán, alias Mobhaoi, patron of Cloney in Co. Kildare, first accompanied Crónán to Assaroe in Co. Donegal to read the scriptures there (§2), and later allegedly died at Lusmagh (§11).[3]

Unlike Ruadhán of Lorrha, whose feast was marked by four lines of encomium in Aonghas of Tallaght's metrical martyrology, compiled about 830, Crónán received no more than a one-line reference to his quality of 'firmness'.[4] The greater part of the quatrain for Crónán's feastday of 28 April was reserved for Christopher and the many martyred with him. The Martyrology of Tallaght, however, of which Aonghas was also the probable author, gave Crónán first place in its list of Irish saints, together with a reference to the saint's otherwise rarely used alias Mochua.[5]

Several later texts, not associated with Roscrea, find room for Crónán. Among these is the Life of Molua of Clonfertmulloe which gave Crónán, then allegedly in Monaincha, the signal honour of rendering the last rites to its

1 Ó Riain, *Corpus*, §225; *DIS* 234–5. A note added to *MartO* 118 attaches the saint to the 'Moccu Éle'. For a detailed account of Éile and its peoples, see Cunningham, *The Anglo-Norman advance*, 13–23. According to the pedigree of the Uí Mheachair, Crónán's successor was entitled to tribute from each lord of the family, as well as the honour of officiating at his inauguration (Pender, 'The O'Clery Book of genealogies', §2046). 2 Grosjean, 'Poems on St Senan', 94 §10. 3 Ó Riain, *Corpus*, §722.22. According to the martyrologies, Baodán died on the same day as Colum of Terryglass: *MartO* 251; *MartG* 238. See also *DIS* 85–6. 4 *MartO* 109. 5 *MartT* 37. 6 *VSHP* ii, 223 §52.

5 The gable end and Romanesque doorway of the medieval church at Roscrea (image © National Monuments Service, Department of the Arts, Heritage and the Gaeltacht).

subject.[6] This honour may have been prompted by Molua's status as co-patron of the diocese of Killaloe, which had either reabsorbed Roscrea or was intent on doing so. Monaincha likewise formed the background to the saint's mention in the Life of Mochuda of Lismore, who, having refused to accept the hospitality offered him at a place located in a 'deserted bog', caused Crónán to move to Roscrea; a variant version of this episode is found at §17 below.[7] A poem attributed to Cuana, king of the Fir Mhaighe in north Cork, remarks that Crónán 'loved not niggardliness', and a poem in Classical Irish cites 'steadfast' Crónán, possibly of Roscrea, together with numerous other saints, among those called upon to help in releasing Ireland's southern half (Leath Mhogha) from a bondage imposed on it by the northern half of Ireland, represented by Finnian of Clonard.[8]

Little is recorded of local devotion to Crónán in the period that followed the completion of the English conquest of Ireland at the end of the sixteenth century. All that John O'Donovan had to say of him following his visit to Roscrea in 1840 was that locals took the image over the doorway of the church to represent Crónán.[9] The local Catholic church, built in 1855, was dedicated to him, as was the Church of Ireland building erected in 1811–13.[10]

Pilgrims would no doubt have flocked annually to Roscrea on the saint's feastday, which fell on 28 April.[11] A week later, on 4 May, a namesake and probable double of the saint, Crónán (alias Mochua) son of Cuimín, was venerated in the Slieve Felim mountains on Limerick's border with Tipperary.[12]

THE CHURCH

Roscrea was an early church of substance, as may be seen from numerous entries in the pre-Anglo-Norman annals, beginning in 800 with the obit of an abbot named Fianghus, followed by that of his son Díoma in 816.[13] That succession to the abbacy was already hereditary would suggest that Roscrea was by then a *seancheall*, 'old church', at a time when the *céili Dé* were founding many new churches.[14] Roscrea and the neighbouring church of Monaincha nonetheless figure prominently in the literature of that group, with both churches named in the 'Monastery of Tallaght', a ninth-century treatise on *céili Dé* practice, on

7 *VSHP* i, 194 §61.   8 O'Daly, 'Mesce Chúanach', 78 §6; McInerney, 'A poem on the saints of Munster', 17, 19n.   9 *OSLTY* iii, 364.   10 Hayes and Kennedy, *The parish churches*, 209.   11 *MartO* 109; *MartT* 37.   12 *MartO* 122; *MartT* 39.   13 *AU* 800, 816. For list of abbots, see Gwynn and Gleeson, *A history*, 61–2.   14 Follet, *Céli Dé in Ireland*, 90–1; Gwynn and Gleeson, *A history*, 60.

6 Remains of the small
Romanesque church at Monaincha
(image © National Monuments
Service, Department of the Arts,
Heritage and the Gaeltacht).

which Ealáir of Monaincha was allegedly an authority.[15] Similarly, the pride of place given to Crónán in the list for his day (28 April) in the Martyrology of Tallaght, the more or less official calendar of *céili Dé* saints, may reflect the high status of his church within these circles.[16] Also, the late eighth- or ninth-century gospel-book named after Díoma, which is associated with the *céili Dé*, was kept at Roscrea by the coarbs of Crónán.[17]

Roscrea was not spared the effects of Viking depredations. In 845, according to the text on the *War of the Gaedhil with the Gaill*, a great battle took place at the site on the eve of the feast of Peter and Paul, when an *aonach,* 'fair', was in progress there.[18] The 'foreigners' were allegedly defeated in the battle and 'countless numbers' of them were slain. As the feast of Peter and Paul is unlikely to have been marked by a fair before the arrival in Roscrea in the mid-twelfth century of the external order of canons regular of St Augustine, who were particularly devoted to the two apostles, doubt must attach to the circumstances of this battle.[19] In that year, several neighbouring churches, including Clonmacnoise, Clonfert, Terryglass and Lorrha, were burned by Vikings, a list to which Roscrea was added by the author of the above-mentioned text.[20]

Apart from the continuing record of its abbots, little notice is taken of Roscrea in the annals between the ninth and the twelfth century.[21] In the meantime, however, as another sign of substance, a round tower had been added to the church, which was struck by lightning in 1135 (*AFM*).[22] Two years previously, in 1133, the church had been burned by an unidentified human hand, and this was repeated in 1147 and 1154 (*AFM*). Such attacks on churches seem to have been unremitting about this time. Finally, in 1157, Roscrea fell victim to Muircheartach Ua Lochlainn of the Ceinéal Eoghain of Tyrone, then the most powerful ruler in the country, who, having dispensed exemplary largesse to the monks of Mellifont, went on a hosting into Munster during which he 'destroyed Roscrea' (*AFM*).

Despite the damage that must have been done to the fabric of the church, about this time Roscrea was pursuing the even higher status of an episcopal see. This status was granted to it at the synod of Kells-Mellifont in 1152, according to the diocesan list drawn up by the papal legate, Cardinal Paparo.[23] The diocese was based on the kingdom of Éile, an area equivalent to the present

---

15 MT §§4–5.   16 Follet, *Céli Dé in Ireland*, 160–1; *MartT* 37.   17 Follet, *Céli Dé in Ireland*, 160–1.
18 Todd, *Cogadh Gaedhel re Gallaibh*, 14 §15.   19 Gwynn and Hadcock, *Medieval religious houses*, 162.
20 *AU* 845.3; Todd, *Cogadh Gaedhel re Gallaibh*, 16 §17.   21 Bhreathnach, 'Who controlled Roscrea?',
36–7; Mc Carthy, 'Collation of annalistic entries'.   22 See now Cunningham, *The round tower at Roscrea*.
23 Ó Cíobháin, 'Deoisí na hÉireann', 52–6.

Offaly baronies of Ballybritt and Clonlisk and Tipperary baronies of Eliogarty and Ikerrin, and its first bishop, Isaac Ua Cuanáin, a member of Crónán's coarbial family, died in 1161.[24] As has been suggested by Aubrey Gwynn, the bishop may have marked his appointment by taking the biblical name Isaac in place of the native form Eachtghus, as a poem of eighty-six quatrains on the Eucharist, probably written about this time, is attributed to Eachtghus Ua Cuanáin.[25] Roscrea appears, however, to have had little opportunity to assert its episcopal status; after Isaac only one other bishop is known, a man named Ua Cearbhaill who died in 1168.[26] Like Scattery Island, which also figures among the new sees established at Kells-Mellifont, Roscrea had been reabsorbed into the diocese of Killaloe by the end of the twelfth century.

During its brief period of high status, Roscrea probably underwent many improvements, including the erection of a high cross, depicting either a bishop or an abbot, and the building of a church with an impressive Romanesque doorway that has been dated to the twelfth century.[27] Moreover, as often happened when change was pending, a Life may also then have been compiled for Crónán in support of Roscrea's bid for episcopal status.[28]

THE LIFE

Written in Latin, Crónán's Life, in common with most other Irish saints' Lives, has yet to be studied critically.[29] As was customary in saints' Lives, this begins with an account of the saint's parents; his father Odhrán is said to have belonged to the people of Éile, whereas his mother Caoimhre is assigned to the people of Corca Bhaiscinn, now roughly the equivalent of the south-west Clare baronies of Clonderalaw and Moyarta.[30] As members of the Uí Chearbhaill family, beginning with Giolla Pádraig (d. 1022) son of Cearbhall, mainly enjoyed the kingship of Éile, it was doubtless this connection that the saint's biographer had in mind.[31] According to the corpus of saints' genealogies,

---

24 *AFM s.a.*; Gwynn and Hadcock, *Medieval religious houses*, 95–6.   25 Gwynn and Gleeson, *A history*, 73–8. As pointed out in Boyle, 'Echtgus Úa Cúanáin's poetic treatise', 185n, this identification, while possible, is not certain.   26 *AI* 1168.3; Gwynn and Hadcock, *Medieval religious houses*, 96. As *AI* records his death in Lismore and *AFM* refers to Ross Carbery rather than Roscrea, some doubt attaches to this entry.   27 Farrelly and O'Brien, *Archaeological inventory*, §1843; Harbison, *The high crosses*, i, 162–3; Ó Carragáin, *Churches in early medieval Ireland*, 43.   28 Gwynn and Gleeson, *A history*, 63; Cunningham, *The Anglo-Norman advance*, 44.   29 *VSHP* ii, 22–31; *VSHH* 274–9; cf. Kenney, *Sources*, 460; O'Hanlon, *The Lives*, iv, 516–24; Bhreathnach, 'Who controlled Roscrea?', 33–5; Ó Riain, 'The medieval story', 158–62.   30 *VSHP* ii, 22 §1.   31 *AI* 1022.

Crónán's mother was a daughter of Niall son of Meachar of the Uí Chonaire of Loop Head.[32] Meachar's uncle, Bolg, is supposed to have been blessed by Patrick, and this might be thought to have provided good reason for choosing this Corca Bhaiscinn family as suitable background for Crónán's mother.[33] Unfortunately, although specified in Crónán's Life as 'cella filiorum Odrani', the church in Corca Bhaiscinn named after the saint and his brother (or brothers), if it ever existed, can no longer be identified.

About the time that Roscrea was seeking diocesan status, so also was Scattery Island, whose jurisdiction would have corresponded approximately to the territory of Corca Bhaiscinn.[34] Bishops of both Roscrea and Scattery are included in the list of attendees at the synod of Kells-Mellifont drawn up by Cardinal Paparo in 1152.[35] It could be, therefore, that Crónán's mother was assigned to the Corca Bhaiscinn as an expression of solidarity between Roscrea and Scattery in their efforts to break free from the diocese of Killaloe, which they had formed part of since the synod of Rathbrassil in 1111.

A concern with diocesan issues may also underlie the frequent references in the Life to property donations in or near Éile, with particular reference to the saint's sojourn at the Offaly church of Lusmagh, the focus of nine chapters (§§7–16). Although still patron of Lusmagh, albeit under the anglicized guise of Cronin, neither the saint's church in Roscrea, nor the diocesan church of Killaloe, has any claim to jurisdiction over it.[36] Now part of the diocese of Clonfert, Lusmagh parish is anomalous in that it is the only one located east of the River Shannon.[37] This raises the possibility that the parish was at one time a bone of contention between Roscrea and Clonfert, which would explain the clear concern of Crónán's biographer with the site, and his emphasis on the fact that, because of the demons that inhabited the place, no one could live there until the saint expelled them (§10). Through Crónán's primary occupancy of the site, Roscrea may have been arrogating to itself a claim to authority over Lusmagh. Similarly, while at Lusmagh, Crónán is said to have

32 Ó Riain, *Corpus*, §§132, 697.3. Another, much later, source assigns the role of mother to Inghean Bhaoith of Killinaboy (Grosjean, 'Poems on St Senan', 94). Meachar is probably the man described in the pedigrees of the Corca Bhaiscinn as a son of Conaire (whence Uí Chonaire): O'Brien, *Corpus*, 324g50–5. As such, he was also a forefather of Uidhre the bishop (*DIS* 580). 33 Stokes, *Lives of the saints*, 1800–12; *VSHP* ii, 22 §1. 34 Gwynn and Hadcock, *Medieval religious houses*, 96–7. 35 Ó Cíobháin, 'Deoisí na hÉireann', 52–6. 36 When visited by Thomas O'Conor in 1838 in the course of the Ordnance Survey, Lusmagh appears to have been giving preference to another putative first cousin of Crónán, Mochonna (alias Mochoinne) who gave name to Kilmochonna, now a townland but then thought to have been the original name of the parish (*OSLOY* i, 199; Lewis, *Topographical dictionary*, ii, 325; *VSHP* ii, 22 §2). 37 See Cunningham, *The Anglo-Norman advance*, 23, 27 (n. 52).

7 Stone cross at Monaincha, with traces of interlace and a weathered figure of Christ crucified (image © National Monuments Service, Department of the Arts, Heritage and the Gaeltacht).

been joined by Mobhaoi, his first cousin through his mother Caoimhre, and therefore also maternally of the Corca Bhaiscinn (§11).[38] Wishing to leave the place for his church in the lands of the Leinstermen (later Cloney in the parish of Kilberry, on Kildare's modern boundary with Laois), Mobhaoi was advised to remain in Lusmagh, where he died a few days later, thus providing Crónán's devotees in Roscrea with a further claim to Lusmagh, through the death there of their patron's first cousin. Among the many miracles attributed to Crónán in Lusmagh was one connected with the miraculous production of the Book of Díoma, now in the library of Trinity College Dublin (§9).[39] As this was kept at Roscrea, possibly as one of the saint's *insignia*, the claim that it had been written at Lusmagh would also have served to strengthen Roscrea's right to jurisdiction over the site.

Arguably, then, the main purpose in having a Life written for Crónán was the support its contents would provide for Roscrea's diocesan ambitions. But this may not have been the sole aim of the biographer. Lusmagh and other properties allegedly granted to Crónán, among them Ráith Eidhin (now possibly Rathavin in the parish of Rathcool, barony of Middlethird), may have been impropriate to Roscrea under another heading, represented by its priory of canons regular of St Augustine.[40]

The text of the saint's Life shows a considerable interest in the affairs of Monaincha (earlier Loch Cré) in the parish of Corbally. The founding of Seanros, near Monaincha, is described (§16), as is the move from there to the 'public way' at Roscrea itself (§17). Although both Roscrea and Monaincha were long-established sites, with each receiving mention in documents from the ninth century or even earlier, nowhere else in the previous record are they brought together in relation to one person and the community that recognized him as head.[41] It seems likely, therefore, that the union of interest between Roscrea and Monaincha underlying their treatment in the Life was the presence in both communities of the canons regular of St Augustine, who appear to have arrived in the area about 1140.[42] A link with the affairs of the canons would also explain the time allegedly spent by Crónán and his cousin Mobhaoi in Clonmacnoise (§§5–6), where there was a house of Augustinian canons, and also one of canonesses, possibly founded before 1146.[43] What may well be a veiled reference to the canons regular is the prophecy then attributed to

38 Ó Riain, *Corpus*, §§697.1–3, 722.22.   39 *VSHP* ii, 24 §9; *VSHH* 276 §8; TCD MS 59. Gwynn and Gleeson, *A history*, 64–71.   40 Ó Cearbhaill, *Cluain i Logainmneacha*, 67.   41 *AU* 807, 839, 859.   42 Gwynn and Hadcock, *Medieval religious houses*, 187–8, 192.   43 Ibid., 165.

Ciarán that, though Crónán's church would be rich and charitable, that of Mobhaoi would be marked by observation of a rule (Latin *regula*, whence regular) and communal custom (*communem consuetudinem*).[44]

The relatively short Life of Crónán ends with an account of his death and burial, which are described in formulaic terms similar to those in other such texts. Due emphasis is given to Roscrea's possession of his remains and, no doubt with a view to attracting pilgrims, to the continuing efficacy of his relics.[45]

MANUSCRIPTS AND PREVIOUS EDITIONS

The Life survives in two Latin recensions, one represented by the Marsh's Library, Dublin, MS Z.3.1.5 (M, formerly *Kilkenniensis*) and Trinity College Dublin, MS E.iii.11 (T) collections, the other by the Salamancan collection (S, *Salmanticensis*), now in the Bibliothèque Royale, Brussels (Bibliothèque Royale MS 7672–4). Both recensions cover much the same ground, but S truncates considerably, omitting much onomastic detail, and ends abruptly at §26, without any obvious break in the manuscript. The Salamancan version has been published in *Acta sanctorum* (Apr. iii, 580–3), again in De Smedt and De Backer, *Acta sanctorum Hiberniae*, 541–50 and, more recently, in *VSHH* 274–9.[46] The present translation is based on the Marsh's Library version, which has been edited by Charles Plummer in *VSHP* ii, 22–31.

---

44 See note to §5.   45 *VSHP* ii, p. 31 §29.   46 It ends with a chapter corresponding to *VSHP* ii, 30 §26.

The Life of Crónán of Roscrea

Here begins the Life of holy Crónán, bishop and confessor

1 ~   The glorious Abbot Crónán was a native of the province of Munster. His father Odhrán belonged to the people of Éile, and lived in that region, not far from the cairn of An Mhagh, with a wife belonging to the people of Corca Bhaiscinn, which lies on the western shore of Munster, facing the ocean. Called Caoimhre, she bore her husband three children, one of whom was that Crónán whose Life we wish to make briefly known to you. When persecution of Odhrán, Crónán's father, by the ruler of the kingdom of Éile broke out, he and his people were expelled from their inheritance. At that, he came with his wife and children to the aforesaid region of Corca Bhaiscinn, because his wife was from there, and, while living there, they founded the church of the sons of Odhrán.

2 ~   From the cradle, Crónán, God's elected one, carried fear and love of the Lord in his breast. Leaving behind his parents as well as their possessions, he went away to read the holy Scriptures and be taught ecclesiastical discipline by holy fathers. He had as companion on the journey a holy and modest man by the name of Mobhaoi, a son of Cualde and the sister of Crónán's mother; Crónán's mother and those of Mobhaoi and Mochoinne were three sisters. Crónán set out then for the province of Connacht and dwelt near Assaroe, where, on hearing of his devoutness, good men came to him and took monastic vows.

3 ~   One day, as Crónán was out in the countryside, he saw a certain bound man being led to his death by a king. Crónán interceded with the king on behalf of the man, asking that he be discharged to himself, but the proud king was unwilling to listen to the holy man of the Lord. Bound hand and foot, that unfortunate man was then thrown into the depths of Assaroe at the command of the king but, after he had been bound in this way under water in the deepest

lake for a great part of the day, the king and his people, while still there on the shore, saw him coming quickly to land. The king then interrogated him as to what had happened to him, and he replied: 'Crónán held me in his lap while I was under water, and kept me from harm so that I experienced no ill; after a while, however, he lifted me up in his lap and brought me to this place, as you see me'. On hearing this, the king came to Crónán and, repenting, bent his knee in his presence before handing over that man free to him. The holy man then blessed the king, and all who were there glorified the power of Christ in his servants.

4 ~   Crónán remained in Connacht and, like a most prudent bee, collected honey there, that is to say the sweetness of religion and piety. On a certain day, when he and his disciples were walking in that region, they saw a huge grave on the way, and the brethren, marvelling at that, said: 'If the man lying in that grave were to greet us alive, he could tell us much about many invisible things'. On hearing this, Crónán said to them: 'Children, God is capable of granting that to you'. Blessing the grave, Crónán then ordered the one lying in it to rise up for them obediently in the name of Christ. Immediately, a man of wondrous size rose up from the grave and, while residing obediently in their presence, he narrated much for them. He told them also about his pagan acts and about the place he occupied in hell, before asking to be baptized. The holy man then baptized him and commanded him to die immediately. Dying a believer, he was buried there in peace.

5 ~   At a certain time, when both Crónán and Mobhaoi were with Ciarán's community in the monastic town of Clonmacnoise, Crónán used to take the leftovers of his food with him to give to the poor in the name of Christ, whereas Mobhaoi used to send it to the assembly of the brethren. On hearing of this, the holy abbot of the monastery said prophetically to all: 'There will always be this difference between the churches of Crónán and Mobhaoi; Crónán's church will have both riches and charity, whereas Mobhaoi's will truly have observation of a rule and communal custom'. And thus it is in their communities.

6 ~   Another day in the same monastic town, namely Clonmacnoise, holy Crónán had been praying alone in a hut when there came to him some lepers who, on seeing the saint praying within, stood outside because they did not wish to hinder his prayer. Knowing this, holy Crónán prayed for them until there

was a great fall of rain. In proven faith, the lepers washed themselves in the water that dripped from Crónán's hut, and the saint's prayer inside greatly benefitted those outside. For, by washing themselves in that water, the lepers' most foul leprosy was cleansed in that place, and their flesh became as that of a beautiful youth. Seeing that their bodies were clean, they gave thanks to God and Crónán, and they told everyone throughout the town how they had been cleansed.

7 ~ Thereafter, Crónán departed from that community and began to build churches in honour of the Lord, as he did from the beginning of his life until his death but, because of his great charity, he left almost all of those churches, with all their possessions, to other saints looking for a place. He came then to that place which is called Lusmagh (that is to say, a fragrant plain), where he remained for a long time, performing many miracles.

8 ~ One day, when the servant of God was in a nearby wood, he saw a passing deer, which he called over to him. The deer came most meekly to Crónán and ate apples agreeably from the saint's lap before departing placidly on its way with the permission and command of the saint.

9 ~ The blessed father Crónán asked of a certain scribe that he make a copy of the four gospels for him. As the scribe, Díoma by name, was willing to write for one day only, the saint said to him: 'Write without a break until the sun will have set on you'. The scribe promised to do so and the saint set up a writing seat for him, but both the grace of Crónán and divine power made the sun shine continuously in this place for forty days and nights during which the scribe was neither weary, nor uninterested, nor troubled by a desire for food, drink or sleep, for he thought that the space of forty days and nights was as one day only. He copied the four gospels during this time and, on the same day, he noticed it to be night and felt hungry. When both the religious and Crónán informed him that he had written for the space of forty days and nights without darkness, he and all who were there gave thanks to the power of Christ.

10 ~ In the aforesaid place – Lusmagh in the region of Múscraighe Tíre – there was an innumerable multitude of demons that filled everywhere as if it were their own home so that no one had been able to live there before Crónán. Holy father Crónán then went bravely into battle with them in the name of

Almighty God and, through the grace of Christ, ejected them from the place until the end of the world. From that day on, they neither do harm nor show themselves there.

11 ~ At a certain time, Mobhaoi wished to depart from Crónán, then in Lusmagh, to his own church in the lands of the Leinstermen. Crónán said prophetically to him: 'Do not, dear one in Christ, depart from here because you will not reach your own place alive but, where your feet now rest, you will die after a few days'. Which is what happened, for afterwards Mobhaoi became ill, and he departed for Christ at the aforesaid place. His small, blessed body was then transported by Crónán to his own church in the lands of the Leinstermen.

12 ~ At another time, a certain deaf man named Osán came to Crónán and requested hearing from him in the name of Christ. Upon Crónán praying for the man, his ears were immediately opened, and he was able to hear. While greatly glorifying the grace of God in Crónán, this man joyously went on his way.

13 ~ In the springtime, when Crónán's brethren had neither a horse nor oxen with which to cover with earth the seed scattered in the field, holy father Crónán himself, drawing beyond the strength of eight, began to cover the seed. The Lord, taking pity on him, then made two of the king of Tara's horses come on their own to finish the work, but the drivers of the horses came after them and led them back to the king. Fleeing once more, those horses returned to Crónán and, on hearing of this, the king of Tara made a gift of them to the saint. Perceiving this to be a gift from God, the holy man gave thanks to the Saviour.

14 ~ In a certain year, when Crónán's monks had no refection for the Easter feast, they said to him: 'Father, request for us some refection of the Lord for his holy Easter feast'. The holy man said to them: 'Our Lord God is rich, and he will grant us children the necessities'. This is what happened in truth because, on Holy Saturday, Crónán's relatives came with alms from their lands. While they were on their way, as yet some distance from Crónán's church, they heard the sound of a bell for vespers and, lest they should travel either after Easter vespers or on Sunday, they sat on the bank of the River Brosna not far from the church until Monday. They came then on Monday to Crónán and bestowed on him in alms as much as sufficed until Pentecost for God's saint, his disciples and guests.

15 ~ At another time, a net belonging to Crónán's monks was immersed in the depths of the River Shannon. In order to avoid lack of chasteness, Crónán did not wish to have his monks naked while raising the net from out of the depths; so, as nine laymen were standing on the riverbank, he asked that they raise the net by swimming. Being proud in themselves, however, all except one did not wish to obey the saint. On that same day, those proud warriors were slain by their enemies rushing at them, save only the one who obeyed Crónán. As his opponent raised his hand with a sword to cut off the head of the unwary one, the terrified man said: 'In Crónán's name, allow me to leave unharmed'. The hand immediately withered without movement, and the aforesaid man escaped from the danger, the others being killed. He then came to Crónán, and stayed with him in a holy habit until death.

16 ~ After that, some holy monks seeking a place to stay came to Crónán, and in his usual fashion, as already stated, the holy abbot gave them his church of Lusmagh, with all that was in it, for charity's sake. Soon after, as he was departing from the place with the monks, he said to his brethren: 'Which of you stole something from our place?' A certain brother then confessed that he had taken a hoe with him, and Crónán said: 'Go back with your hoe and stay in that place until the day of your death'. The brother, though bewailing the absence of his holy Abbot Crónán, returned out of obedience and stayed in the place until his death. Thereafter, holy Crónán came to his own native place of Éile in the eastern part of Munster, and stayed near the marsh of Lurga by the land of Ossory, which is the western part of Leinster. There he built the church called Seanros at the lake of Cré, in which there is a small island containing a monastery of ever-religious monks. Crónán was in that church for a long time, and many miracles were done by him there.

17 ~ On a certain day, good men who came to Crónán to spend the night in his guesthouse, though searching with much effort for his place, could not find it. The church of the man of God was remote from the level road, with the result that the royal guests spent the night on the road without food or cover. On hearing of this on the following day, Crónán, greatly saddened at the loss of way and cold condition of those guests, but burning with love, summoned a certain boy who used to carry vessels to the byre for the purpose of bringing milk and butter to the church in a horse and cart, and asked that he lead him secretly to the royal highway. This being agreed, Crónán went into the cart and hid among the vessels. Then, with nobody else knowing, the boy took

him to the place on the royal highway at which the above-mentioned guests had spent the previous night. Sitting there, he said to the boy: 'Return to your work, but I'll remain here'. On hearing that, the monks went out after him to ask that he return to his own place, but holy Abbot Crónán said: 'I shall not be in a remote place where neither guests nor the poor can find me easily; instead, I'll stay here on the public way, where they will be able to find me, and I shall serve my Lord Christ, the king of kings, in this place'. Still wishing to remain in a more secure church, his monks went to the holy Bishop Fursa so that, coming with them, he too might ask Crónán to return to his own place. Blessed Bishop Fursa said: 'I shall not move your holy abbot from the place he has chosen, for just as bees take care of their hives on a summer day, so also the visitation of angels about his place does not cease, and over it the door of heaven is open. Go, therefore, preferably to your abbot and obey him'. Crónán's brethren then came to him, bringing with them from the church of Seanros a surplice and some clothes on their shoulders. The holy senior Crónán built a great monastery in that place, and a famous monastic town called Roscrea grew up there, in which Crónán reposed in Christ after many miracles.

18 ~ Once, the people of Ossory came to lay waste the territory of Éile, and its people fled for refuge to Crónán so that he might protect them. Crónán's monks were really in great fear, but he said to them: 'Do not fear, because this inimical army will do no harm here, however much they will imagine they have done'. Which is what happened, because that army thought it had killed many men, laid waste the land, set houses on fire and then, with great victory and jubilation, returned to its own lands. But a wondrous thing was done there by the great power of God through Crónán's merits, because, after they returned to their own country, all the people of Éile were found to be safe; no house there had been burned, nor had any animal perished, and nobody had been killed, except one only who failed to come with the others to Crónán. The grace of God not only protected Crónán's place, but also all the people for whom the saint himself prayed, whereas it appeared to the people of Ossory as a mirage of destruction. From this, Crónán's reputation spread widely through various regions.

19 ~ Once, when Mochaomhóg who ruled over the monastery of Leigh arrived with many others, Crónán made him a large meal from few resources, for the saint, being bountiful and charitable, held back nothing of material things.

The cellarer of the monastery had nothing that night, except one pitcher of beer, a medium-sized vessel of butter, and a small amount of flour, but when these were brought to Crónán, he blessed them in the name of Christ, and ordered that they be prepared and ministered to the community and guests. At that same meal, with the ingredients increasing through Crónán's blessing, 120 men ate their fill, as much as they wanted. While thus eating long into the night, a certain lay-brother said out loud: 'I feel already that matins will not be celebrated tonight in this place'. Crónán, however, replied: 'Brother, one receives Christ in a guest; we ought, therefore, to rejoice in the coming of Christ and have a meal and, if you had not spoken, the angels of God would have prayed in our places this night'. Afterwards, the banquet came to an end and, blessing his gifts, the holy men gave thanks to God.

20 ~ At a certain time, Colmán son of Miodhghna was seriously ill in a castle called Ráith Eidhin, and sent for Crónán to come to his passing away. Crónán set out on the way but, before he came, the lord Colmán died and was lifeless for a day and night. On arrival, Crónán turned outside all the others and prayed on his own near the cold corpse, at which Colmán immediately arose safe from the dead and greeted the saint. Seeing him alive, his people raised a shout in praise of God, and Colmán, who surrendered himself and his seed after him forever to God and to Crónán, lived bodily for an entire year.

21 ~ Crónán resuscitated another man called by the name of Colmán, who had been slain by his enemies. Crónán performed this miracle at the doorway of a fort called Ráith Fhiodhalta, where, with the saint praying for him, the slain man immediately arose healthily from the dead in front of all. Afterwards, he lived on for seven years and, while blessing his Saviour, he offered himself up to Crónán.

22 ~ Once when the holy elder Crónán, accompanied by a lone driver, was going in a wagon to the lands of Corca Mhoicheine, the driver spotted a large piece of wood lying across the road. He said to the elder: 'What shall we do, father, since we cannot pass by with the wagon on the road because of this timber'. Crónán said: 'Place your head meanwhile in my lap, son', and when he had done so the timber suddenly rose up, and did not fall back down for many years, until it weakened through decay. Nine laymen of the seed of Aoldobhar, who secretly witnessed this miracle from the side of the road, came to Crónán and, having offered themselves to him and to God forever, they were made monks.

23 ~ On a certain day, when guests came to Crónán, he ordered the brethren to give them food and beer. One brother, however, said: 'The beer that we have, father, is certainly not yet fermented, and we cannot pour an inferior one'. Crónán replied: 'The upper lips of the cask are surely wider than the lower opening. Bring, therefore, from the cask a drink for the guest as if to Christ, for the Lord is capable of putting strength in the liquor'. A vessel was then filled up with beer from the cask and immediately, through divine will, the liquor became fully fermented so that, on drinking it, the guests became greatly inebriated. The compassion, then, of the man of God quickly made beer that was not yet fermented so full of strength that it intoxicated men, and those who knew of this gave praise to Christ.

24 ~ At another time, Fínghein, king of Munster, went into the region of Éile and made camp there at a fort called Ráith Bheagáin. A certain thief then came from the region of Midhe and stole two of the king's horses, whereupon the king, greatly incensed, wanted to strike an intolerable blow on Éile, thinking that it was its inhabitants who had stolen his horses. On hearing of this, and having been asked by many, Crónán made his way to the king in order to lessen his anger, at which the king's steward was gripped by a great pain, and so hugely tormented by it that he could not at all sleep but wailed incessantly. His inflated stomach then swelled so inordinately that the king's friends appealed to the holy elder Crónán on his behalf. At this, the saint sent his belt to him, and once this was placed around the loins of the sick man, the swelling of his belly disappeared immediately. That same hour, the steward came healed and unharmed to the king and, on hearing and seeing him, Fínghein dismissed through Crónán all that was owed to him by the inhabitants of Ráith Bheagáin, who had been supposed to guard his horses. But Crónán also wished to satisfy the king and, lo and behold, two piebald horses with golden reins came directly out of the lake of Cré and stood meekly in front of the saint. Crónán presented these to the king, and the superb horses placed their tamed necks under the king's chariot, leaving him very joyful at Crónán's gifts and blessings.

25 ~ This same king Fínghein had a deaf and dumb son named Maonach who was taken privately, at the command of his father, to be blessed by Crónán. On the holy father greeting and blessing the boy, he – now hearing well – immediately spoke, giving thanks to his Saviour. The king and his chieftains thereupon honoured the holy elder Crónán and his church.

26 ~ Another time, a gospel-book, when opened by Crónán, fell into the lake of Cré, and was in the depths of the lake for forty days and nights. Crónán, who frequently dwelt in the aforementioned island on the lake, grieved greatly at this. Moreover, when the gospel-book was found through divine will and the grace of the man of God, not a letter in it was lost, despite much time under water. To this day that gospel-book remains honoured in Crónán's monastery.

27 ~ A golden apple, with two golden chains hanging from it, was once found in the fort called Cluain Earc. The inhabitants of the place, knowing that it was a royal gift, made a bronze apple similar to it, with two chains gilded carefully on the outside, because they feared that the king of Cashel would rightfully take the find from them. On hearing about it, the king sent his prefect, who said to them: 'Where is the royal gift that was found among you. Give it to the king so that he may have his due'. They then gave him the bronze they had made, and this was brought to the king. At that time, the holy elder Crónán was in the town of Cashel with the king, but already, because of old age, the eyes of the most blessed father could see nothing. As the bronze was going from hand to hand through the palace of the king, being viewed by people, it was placed in the hand of the holy elder who, on feeling it, said prophetically in front of all: 'This here is not what was found earlier in the fort of Cluain Earc. What happened is that the finders deceitfully made a gilded bronze in place of the gold'. Thereupon, on the king testing the prophecy, as told by the saint, it was found to be so, and when the bronze piece had been broken up, the king sent again to the inhabitants of the aforesaid fort, who, now forced by the messengers, handed over the royal gift. On learning about this, the king and all others marvelled at Christ's grace as in his holy elder Crónán, and afterwards, now honoured by both king and all the people, feeble Crónán returned full of piety from the town of Cashel to his monastic town of Roscrea.

28 ~ The little that has been said here of the virtues of the most holy elder, our Crónán, and the little said of the miracles which Christ performed through him, I wrote, dearest brethren, for your honour. This servant of Christ excelled unbelievably more fully than us lukewarm ones from birth to feeble old age, obeying divine commands in mercy, patience, modesty, fasts, prayers, humility and, more than all else, in compassion.

29 ~ When, therefore, his last day had drawn near, Crónán, infirm in body but sound of mind, called his own people to him and, by way of instruction, urged that they remain firm until the end in the good begun by them, while always preserving unity and peace. With his hand raised, he blessed them and their place and, having received the divine sacrament, he died in peace in the most venerable old age on 28 April. He was buried with due honour in his own town of Roscrea in which God's miracles will be performed for all time through his relics. Meanwhile, our Crónán himself departed to Christ among the choirs of angels with untold joy and the sweetest songs. Honour and glory is his with God the father and the Holy Ghost forever and ever. Amen.

The Life of holy Crónán, abbot and confessor, ends.

The Life of Mochaomhóg of Leigh

THE SAINT

MOCHAOMHÓG BELONGED, according to the genealogists, to the Conmhaicne, whose settlements were mainly in Connacht.[1] His father, reputedly a *saor*, 'craftsman', was named Beoán and his mother, Neas, is said to have been a sister of Íde of Killeedy.[2] Supposedly born about the same time as Molua of Kyle (AD554), and provided by the annalists with an obit of 656, the saint is nonetheless also credited with having attained a biblical age of over 400.[3] Commemorated in first place in the lists for his feastday of 13 March, Mochaomhóg is one of few Conmhaicne saints to have become attached to a Munster church. In Ossory, he was remembered at Kilmakevoge in the Kilkenny barony of Ida, a place that later became impropriate to the Augustinian canonesses of Kilculliheen.[4] In Connacht, a site named Cros Mochaomhóg in the Mayo parish of Cong, within the former territory of Conmhaicne Cúile, may recall the saint. Together with Iarlaithe, Cruimhthear Fraoch, and Caillín, Mochaomhóg was hailed as an *ardnaomh*, 'chief saint', of the Conmhaicne, who allegedly owed him tribute.

As an indication of his continuing popularity in east Munster, Mochaomhóg's genealogy was added to a manuscript written in the early fifteenth century for James Butler, the White Earl.[5] Mochaomhóg's feastday of 13 March was also twice used as a point of reference by the compiler of the Annals of Ulster in entries for the years 1109 and 1119.[6] His name, which figures among those mentioned as guardians in the so-called *lorica* of Colum Cille, found its way under the guise of both Mochomogus and Kevoca into Greven's version of the Martyrology of Usuard, compiled in Cologne in the late fifteenth century.[7] The saint's head reputedly formed part of Adhamhnán's reliquary.[8]

---

1 Ó Riain, *Corpus*, §362. 2 Ibid., §722.48. 3 *MartT* 98. The annals entry refers to him under the guise of Caomhán Léith. 4 Carrigan, *The history and antiquities*, iv, 92–3. 5 Macalister, *Book of Fenagh*, 68, 88. 6 Cf. Walsh, *Irish leaders*, 466–7. 7 *Acta sanctorum* (Iun.vi, 153). The form Kevoga, with feminine ending, was borrowed from the Breviary of Aberdeen which had transformed the saint into a fictitious female. 8 Carney, 'A Maccucáin', 35 §15. 9 *AU* 656, 752, 870; *AFM* 655, 746, 838, 868, 900,

THE CHURCH

The church of Leigh – Liath Mór, more fully Liath Mór Mochaomhóg,
anglicized Leamokevoge – in the parish of Twomileborris, barony of Eliogarty,
attracted moderate attention from the annalists. Mochaomhóg's death in 655
(at an advanced age) is noted and six of his successors are named, the last two
of whom held joint abbacies, one at Emly, the other at Longfordpass (Doire
Mór).[9] One early successor, named Cuanghas Caoch, 'purblind', who died in
752, is described as both scribe and abbot.[10] Furthermore, this man's name
figures, together with that of Mochaomhóg, in the list of those commemorated
on 13 March, the two saints of Leigh accounting for an entire quatrain in the
Martyrology of Aonghas.[11] This is an indication that, despite its absence from
other texts associated with the group, Leigh was a *céili Dé* foundation.

The church was among those plundered by Vikings in the middle of the
ninth century, according to *The War of the Gaedhil with the Gaill*.[12] Plundered
with it, according to the same text, were Lorrha and Roscrea. There were two
early churches on the site, one large, the other small, and the remains of a
round tower. It has been suggested that the church was patronized by the Dál
gCais in their struggle with the Eoghanacht of Cashel, and that Brian Bóramha
may have supported the building of one or more of the churches on the site.[13]

Following the beginning of the Anglo-Norman conquest in 1169, Leigh
disappeared completely from the annals.[14]

THE LIFE

Mochaomhóg was deemed important enough to be made the subject of a Life
preserved in both a Latin version and an Irish translation. Perhaps because of
the relatively unimportant status of the saint's church at Leigh, the Life has
attracted little attention, with one commentator dismissing it as 'evidently
late and largely fictitious', a judgment that could be applied to the vast majority
of Irish saints' Lives, without diminishing their importance as historical
documents.[15] In Mochaomhóg's case, although the Life awaits a critical edition,

933, 1014. Cf. Colgan, *Acta sanctorum*, 598 (iv).   10 *AU s.a.*; *AFM* 746.   11 *MartT* 23; *MartO* 82.
12 Todd, *Cogadh Gaedhel re Gallaibh*, 16 §17.   13 Farrelly and O'Brien, *Archaeological inventory*, i,
§1879; Flanagan, *Irish royal charters*, 158–60; Ó Carragáin, *Churches in early medieval Ireland*, 132–3.
14 For a mention in a deed dated to about 1200, see Flanagan, *Irish royal charters*, 312.   15 Kenney,
Sources, 455.

8 Remains of the Cistercian abbey of Kilcooly, in the parish of the same name, Co. Tipperary. The abbey was founded *c*.1182 (image © National Monuments Service, Department of the Arts, Heritage and the Gaeltacht).

there are many pointers to a provenance other than in his own church of Leigh. Chief among these is the manner in which the saint is cast in a deferential pose towards Bishop Colmán, whose church at Longfordpass was located in 'Magh Airbh' (*Arvicampus*), otherwise the name of the Cistercian foundation of Kilcooly.[16] Between Leigh and Longfordpass, within the parish of Kilcooly, there is, as is stated in the Life (§15), little more than four miles.

A Cistercian provenance for Mochaomhóg's Life is also indicated by several other associations established by the saint's biographer, including his resuscitation of a dead man at Inishlounaght (Inis Leamhnachta), near Clonmel, the site of the Cistercian house *de Surio*, which was already founded by 1148 (§32).[17] The saint is also brought on a visit to his 'disciple', Mochoime (Mochuma), patron of the church and parish of Grangemacomb in the barony of Fassadinin, part of the property of the Cistercian house of Jerpoint (§29).[18] Although itself an earlier foundation, Kilcooly became a daughter-house of

16 Gwynn and Hadcock, *Medieval religious houses*, 137–8; Flanagan, *Irish royal charters*, 158–60.   17 Gwynn and Hadcock, *Medieval religious houses*, 135–6.   18 Carrigan, *The history and antiquities*, ii, 322.

Jerpoint in 1184.[19] Accompanying Mochaomhóg on the visit to Mochoime
was Féichín, otherwise best known as patron of the Benedictine abbey at Fore,
but Sheffin (from Teach Féichín), a parish lying a short distance from
Grangemacomb, was also dedicated to him.[20]

Despite the saint's paternal link with Connacht, his biographer describes
how he was born to Neas at her sister's church of Killeedy in south Munster,
where his father was then exercising his craft (§§5–6). This gave the biographer
(§4) the opportunity of attributing, incongruously, a cure of the blindness
affecting Fachtna of Ross Carbery to the miraculous application of Neas's
breast milk, although the infant was as yet unborn. Ross Carbery was the seat
of a Benedictine abbey and nearby was the Cistercian house of Abbeymahon.[21]

For his education, Mochaomhóg is sent to Comhghall at Bangor in Co.
Down (§8). In the twelfth century, Bangor achieved considerable fame through
its connection with the leading church reformer, Maol Maodhóg alias Malachy
– a close friend of Bernard of Clairvaux – who was instrumental in bringing
external orders to Ireland, including the first Cistercian foundation at
Mellifont.[22] This may be yet another indication of Cistercian influence on the
author of Mochaomhóg's Life.

Following his education by Comhghall of Bangor, Mochaomhóg is said to
have returned to Ossory (§§10–11), taking possession on the way of the church
of Anatrim in the Laois parish of Offerlane, before relinquishing it to his
namesake and probable double, Caomhán. This church and its saint also found
mention in the Life of Colum of Terryglass (§13). Among other saints
introduced into Mochaomhóg's Life are Daghán of Ennereilly (§§26–7), Fursa
(§31), Cainneach of Aghaboe (§§18, 25, 27–9), and four fellow pupils of
Comhghall of Bangor, namely Molua, patron of Killaloe and Kyle, Fionnbharr,
Luchtighearn, and Laichtín, the story of whose foundation at Freshford is also
told (§10). Besides their companionship with Mochaomhóg, these saints also
hold in common an association with parochial churches in Co. Kilkenny:
Laichtín at Freshford; Molua at Killaloe; Fionnbharr at various sites, including
Coolcashin and Kilmacahill; and Luchtighearn at Kilkeasy. Some or all of
these churches may have been impropriate to a Cistercian house in the county,
Kilcooly or Jerpoint. Among the lands granted to Jerpoint was Garranamanagh
in 'Congtella' (Aos Cinn Chuille), a name used of the area about Freshford,

19 Gwynn and Hadcock, *Medieval religious houses*, 137.   **20** Carrigan, *The history and antiquities*, ii,
326–7.   **21** Gwynn and Hadcock, *Medieval religious houses*, 107, 125.   **22** Ibid., 66, 116.

which adjoins Garranamanagh.²³ Also adjoining Garranamanagh was Coolcashin, one of the Kilkenny sites associated with Fionnbharr. Towards the end of the Life (§33), the founder of Clashmore (Glais Mhór), near Lismore, is introduced under the guise of Cuán Cearr. As with the name Crónán, traditionally that given to the patron of Clashmore church and parish, Cuán yields a hypocoristic Mochua.

MANUSCRIPTS AND PREVIOUS EDITIONS

The Life survives in Latin and Irish versions, the first in the Marsh's Library, Dublin, MS Z.3.1.5 (M, formerly *Kilkenniensis*) and Trinity College Dublin, MS E.iii.11 (T) collections, the second in Brussels, Bibliothèque Royale, MS 2324–40. The Latin Life has been edited in Colgan, *Acta sanctorum*, 589–99, again in the Bollandist *Acta sanctorum* (Mart. ii, 280–8) and in *VSHP* ii, 164–83, the last of which forms the basis of the translation provided here. The Irish Life has yet to be edited.

---

23 Carrigan, *The history and antiquities*, ii, 258; Ó Riain, Ó Murchadha and Murray, *Historical dictionary*, i, 68.

The Life of Mochaomhóg of Leigh

THE LIFE OF HOLY MOCHAOMHÓG, ABBOT OF LEIGH

The Life of holy Mochaomhóg, bishop and confessor begins

1 ~ The most blessed Abbot Mochaomhóg took his paternal origins from the province of Connacht, namely from the race of Conmhaicne. His father abandoned his home place because of hostility and came to the lands of Munster, where he lived with his family in the country of Uí Chonaill Ghabhra, among the people called Corca Oiche. This man, Beoán by name, was a highly regarded craftsman in timber and stone, and also daring in warfare. He fell in love with a certain beautiful, modest and nobly born woman of the people of the Déise in Munster, a sister of most holy virgin Íde. This woman, Neas by name, wanted to live in permanent chastity, like holy virgins of yore who did not know a man, but her sister, the holy virgin Íde, gave her as wife to the excellent craftsman Beoán. For blessed Íde, God's prophetess, knew this to be divine will.

2 ~ At that time, Beoán the craftsman was constructing a fine building in Íde's monastery and, when done, Íde said: 'Ask a payment, master; what do you want for your work of art?' He replied: 'Promise me in Christ, holy mother, what I shall ask'. When the virgin promised him whatever he might ask, Beoán said to God's saint: 'You know, mother, that your sister, my wife, is barren, and we do not have an heir. Ask of God, therefore, on our behalf, that we may have a son'. The holy virgin said to him: 'You will indeed have a son, chosen before God and men', and this prophecy came to pass in due course.

3 ~ A certain cruel king by the name of Crunnmhaol, from the southern part of Uí Chonaill, gave grave offence to the people of Corca Oiche; he once came with a large army to lay them waste and made a great slaughter of the warriors resisting him, including Beoán the craftsman who was among those beheaded. As she was up to then barren, and they were without heir, Neas came to the carnage with her folk to seek the corpse of her husband, but found the head only, since she could not recognize the body. Bringing the head with her, she

44

showed it, while weeping, to her sister Íde, and said: 'Not this, dear sister, did you promise us, when saying that he would leave a son after him. Behold; since he is dead. my womb will remain closed in its barrenness'. Íde replied: 'Do not weep, sister; God is capable of helping us and fulfilling my promise; go, therefore, and join the head to his body'. Her sister Neas responded: 'We cannot in any case recognize his body, because of the huge amount of blood in the great carnage of the dead'. The holy virgin said, however: 'Call him by name three times in memory of the Holy Trinity, and he will rise and come to you, and when you place the head back on him, he will say: 'O woman, why did you call me; I had it so good'. The woman followed this instruction, and he, strong in spirit and with a body healed and whole, because God's power made it so, repeated to his wife what the holy prophetess Íde had foretold. He and his wife then set out from there together and, on coming to Íde, gave thanks to God on bended knee. Íde then said to him: 'Do you wish to remain, friend, in this life, or go now to Heaven?' Beoán responded: 'I hold this entire world as nothing, like dung, compared with eternal happiness'. Íde then said: 'I think it good, nevertheless, that the payment which I promised should be given back to you'. Íde then washed him with water and afterwards no wound was to be found on him. She blessed him, made him holy, and sent him with his wife to their home; there Beoán slept with his wife and she, with God opening her womb, conceived an esteemed son, full of the grace of God.

4 ~ At that time, the wise and virtuous Fachtna became blind through some occurrence, and could see nothing. This holy man lived near the sea in the southern part of Ireland, in a monastery which he himself founded, and a great monastic town grew up there, Ross Carbery by name, in which there always resided a large group of scholars. The holy man Fachtna then prayed fervently to the Lord so that he might show him a medicine by which to recover his eyesight. Thereafter, an angel of the Lord came to say: 'You will not be able to find a cure for your eyes unless you wash them and your face in the breast milk of the wife of Beoán the craftsman, who has never given birth, but who, by the gift of God, has now conceived a saint in her womb'. Saying this, the angel departed, but the holy man of God did not know either Beoán the craftsman or the region of Ireland in which he lived, and the angel did not resolve it for him. The holy man then said to his people: 'I know what I shall do; I shall go to God's prophetess, blessed Íde, and she will resolve my question'. With that, he made his way to Íde, a journey of five days. When

Fachtna arrived in the territory of Corca Oiche, disciples of his heard men in a mill speaking the name of Beoán the craftsman and, on being questioned as to whether they might be acquainted with the craftsman or know where he lived, one of them said: 'Do you see that woman going into the fort?' When they replied 'We do', he said: 'That is the wife of Beoán the craftsman'. One of them then ran after her, to say: 'Wait a while, happy woman, until our holy elder, who wants to greet you, comes'; and she stayed put, saying: 'In truth, it is a great joy for me that the servant of Christ wishes to greet me'. Then, when Fachtna came, he asked her if she was the wife of Beoán the craftsman, and she responded in her sober and modest way: 'I am, lord'. The saint then said: 'Have you conceived in your womb?' She replied: 'God in his goodness allowed me, sterile one, to do so'. Then, revealing to her his name, the holy man told what had happened to him, but the blessed woman said: 'Lord, my breasts do not yet give milk'. Thereupon, the holy man said: 'In the name of the Holy Trinity, through the sanctity of your child yet to be born, milk them and they will give milk for certain'. When she acted according to the word of the man of God, her breasts poured out milk abundantly and, on washing his eyes in the breast milk of blessed Neas, wife of Beoán the craftsman, the saint recovered his sight in that place. On again seeing heaven and earth clearly, he gave thanks to God, and blessed that woman and her conception. Then, commending to the woman his prayer and the blessing of Íde, he returned with his folk, rejoicing in Christ, to his own monastery.

5 ~   When blessed Neas was close to giving birth, she came with her husband to Íde's monastery, to speak to her. As they were about to return, Neas had birth pangs and sat down in the wagon, at which, having heard the sound of the wagon, Íde said to her folk: 'This wagon is making noise under a king; see whom it runs under'. Returning, the messengers said to God's saint: 'Your sister Neas alone is sitting in the wagon', at which the holy woman said: 'Truly, it makes noise under a king, because, through the grace of God, the boy who is in her womb will sit on high in the kingdom of Heaven'.

6 ~   On coming to her home, Neas gave birth to a boy full of grace and, on the following day, it was announced to Íde that her sister had given birth to a son. The saint rejoiced greatly, saying: 'Whence did Beoán merit having such a son, who will be great before God and men, and forever remembered?' She went on to say: 'He will be beautiful and grow old'. From this, they gave him his first name, Caoimhghin, meaning 'beautiful birth', but God's holy woman

herself overturned this name, preferring to call him by his still popular name, Mochaomhóg, which means in Latin: *meus pulcher iuvenis*, 'my beautiful youth'. From the baptismal font onwards, the grace of God showed itself in him through signs and proofs.

7 ~ One day, his mother, going out, left her little son alone asleep in the cradle and, on looking back, saw a globe of fire rising up from the house. As she ran back quickly to the house, calling out loud, the fire disappeared and did not reappear at all, but she found the happy little boy with a face and form so ruddy that she could neither look at him nor touch him. This is the way in which he was shown to his mother, and all who saw or heard this did not doubt that the fire of the Holy Ghost was visiting the little infant.

8 ~ After this, the boy's father and mother came to Íde, to say: 'Mistress, God's grace is wonderfully apparent in your little boy, our little son, and since he does not suit our carnal ways, he cannot live with us, because we are of the flesh, while he is truly of the spirit'. Íde replied: 'Bring him here, because it falls to me to rear him'. The most blessed abbess then brought him up for God for twenty years in honest manners and in knowledge of letters, and she called him by the name we mentioned above, that is Mochaomhóg, so that he might become a priest and build a church for God. And God's saint foretold that a great community would grow up in his honour in the place in which he would depart for heaven, and Mochaomhóg said to her: 'Let it be done, mother, as you say'. Then, with the permission and blessing of his parents and of his glorious foster-mother, his aunt Íde, Mochaomhóg journeyed to the province of the Ulstermen in the northern part of Ireland, to Comhghall, the holy abbot of many monasteries, taking with him five disciples. Comhghall received him with joy and, before long, Mochaomhóg was ordained priest by him.

9 ~ One day, when Comhghall and Mochaomhóg were praying together, the prior of the monastery in which they then were came to them, to say: 'I marvel greatly, friends of the Lord, at the vision which, by God's leave, I just saw on the road that I came along, and because of it my mind is disturbed by fear and horror. I saw one demon sitting, as if at ease, on the king's fort, while a great throng of demons cruelly stood together, as if ready for battle, around the bounds of our monastery'. God's grace had shown this vision to the prior, but his outward appearance was transformed through fear and horror of the

demons. With holy father Comhghall remaining silent, blessed Mochaomhóg then said: 'Let us rise, father, and give thanks to God, because the brethren uphold the service of God, and a great detestation arises in us when the devil gathers together a throng of demons at our place. Where the devil is served, however, one demon may be seen there at ease, like a provost awaiting his service. Where battle is waged strongly against him, the king sends his warriors with weapons of war, but where there is peace, he sends one messenger only, and in this way the devil also acts towards those who resist him'. The holy elder Comhghall then said: 'What God showed to his servant, you have explained truthfully'. Mochaomhóg replied: 'Rise, father, and let us hold on firmly to our spiritual weapons, and pray that the brethren may witness the demons fleeing from here by the power of Christ, and that by seeing this together with their prior they may trust with us in the Lord. Let you go around the monastery from the left and I from the right, and let us cast out the demons, commanding them in Christ's name not to gather here again until the Day of Judgement'. With the holy men acting in this way, many saw the corrupt demons in flight coming to the fort of the king, where they sat like a garrison and, when the brethren saw and heard of this, they were greatly strengthened in Christ. The fort in which was the king of the Ulstermen is called Rademan, but the monastery in which, it is said, there were three thousand monks in cells under Comhghall's authority is named Bangor.

10 ~ When father Comhghall had seen this, he said to blessed Mochaomhóg: 'Son, you ought to be a father to others and build a place for God where he will point it out to you'. The fathers who, with their disciples, were sent away at the same time by Comhghall so that they might nurture servants of Christ in different parts of Ireland were: holy Mochaomhóg, most blessed Laichtín, who founded the distinguished monastery of Freshford – that is to say 'fresh field', because of the humidity of the little rivers that cross there – and many other churches, Molua son of Oiche, Fionnbharr and Luchtighearn. All of these were found to be upright in Christ Jesus.

11 ~ Mochaomhóg came with his disciples to a place called Anatrim in Slieve Bloom, in the territory of the Leinstermen, and began to build a church there, when a certain secular man came to him, to say: 'Do not work here in vain, because this place will not be yours'. But Mochaomhóg said: 'I shall just stay here until someone, wishing to expel me, takes hold of my hand and drags it'. At this, he took hold of the hand of the man of God, wishing to expel him,

but Mochaomhóg then said: 'What name are you called by?' He replied: 'Brónach is my name'. This means *tristis*, 'sad', in Latin; so the holy man said: 'You have a name appropriate to you because here and in the future you will be sad and, by the will of God, you and your race will be expelled by the chieftain of this kingdom, whereas I shall be in this place until the man of God, Caomhán by name, comes to me, and I shall give the place to him who will be named after it, and whose resurrection will be here'. On hearing this prophecy, and knowing himself to be guilty towards his chieftain, the man angrily retired without penance after the wrongdoing. Everything then happened as the holy man had foretold and, when blessed Caomhán came there, Mochaomhóg handed over the place to him, and Caomhán remained there in great holiness until his death. Mochaomhóg then went on into the territory of Munster.

12 ~ On coming then into Éile in the eastern part of Munster, towards Ossory in the west of the land of the Leinstermen, Mochaomhóg received there a site by the name of Clonmore, from which he went off to greet Caomhán, a powerful lord living nearby in a fort called Rathenny. This man, who had a church within his fort, was both religious and steadfast, and he received the man of God in a friendly manner, and showed him honour. Then, on a certain night, as Mochaomhóg remained for a while in the church, Caomhán's wife looked out from the sun-room and, on seeing every part of the building surrounded by a wall of fire, she called her husband, who saw the same. At that, realizing that they had an extraordinary guest who was being visited by a mission of angels while in the church, they went back and, marvelling, gave thanks to God. On the following day, that man said to Mochaomhóg: 'Lord, we know that you are a man of God and that, with many flocking to you, you will not be able to find in this narrow territory a spacious enough place. So let us both go to my lord, the ruler of the kingdom of Éile, and let him give you a suitable and spacious place'. This pleased the man of God.

13 ~ Before they had come to the ruler, his soothsayer said to him: 'A certain man will come to you today, lord and, if you allow him to dwell in these lands, the power over the territory will fall to him, and he will dominate your kingdom forever'. The ruler responded: 'If he comes to me under arms, I shall bravely resist him, but if he comes in simplicity as a meek preacher of the Christ in whom we believe, he will be pleasing to me'. Mochaomhóg came afterwards with his escort to the fort of the ruler who, on seeing him, became overjoyed

at his arrival and knelt at his feet. Truly, on hearing Mochaomhóg, this ruler, full of the grace of the Holy Spirit, said: 'Behold, O servant of the living God, I am offering you my royal stronghold with everything in it, together with its lands'. The holy man replied: 'We give thanks to God for your kindness, O cultivator of the Christian faith, but I shall not be here, nor will I accept your fortress, but look for a more suitable place in the wilderness, which will please me more'. At this, the ruler said: 'I have a certain secret place in the wilderness, located near the bog of the lake of Lurga, and surrounded by a very dense wood; I offer this to you, if it pleases, together with its boundaries'. As this pleased the holy man of God greatly, the ruler commanded his swineherd, who knew all the remote places well, to lead the saint and his disciples to the aforesaid place, but he refused, saying: 'I cannot go with him, lord, for I ought to search for my many missing pigs, as I do not know what happened to them'. The holy man said: 'Come with me and, when you will have returned, you will find all the pigs which you seek unharmed on the level space in front of this fortress'. Believing the word of the holy man, the swineherd then joyfully went off with him and, when he returned with a blessing, he found his pigs as it had been said to him.

14 ~ When Mochaomhóg arrived at that place, his bell then sounded loudly. Earlier, as he was leaving his foster-mother, the most holy virgin Íde, she had given him a little bell, while saying: 'This bell will be mute, son, until you arrive at the place of your resurrection, where it will sound loudly'. So, on hearing the sound of his bell, the man of God joyfully gave thanks to Christ, knowing that he would arise there from the dead. Mochaomhóg then found in that place, under the shade of a certain tree, a huge, very grey, wild and bristly boar which, setting aside its savageness, stood tamely in front of the holy man of God. The holy man then said to his disciples: 'The name of this place will forever be as in the colour of that boar'. As *canus* in Latin means grey, this place is called by the name *Liath* in the Irish language, and blessed Mochaomhóg first consecrated the place with a three-day fast.

15 ~ Previously, a visitation of angels used to frequent this place, as was shown to the holy Bishop Colmán son of Dáire. He was in his monastery of Doire Mór (that is 'large grove' in Irish, now Longfordpass), which was situated on the confines of Munster and Leinster, but within the region known as Éile in the kingdom of Munster, to whose royal race, the Eoghanacht, the bishop belonged. Now one of the bishop's brethren, while traversing the aforesaid

wood before Mochaomhóg had come there, brought out of it sweet apples which he gave to the holy bishop and, on being asked where the apples had been brought from, he replied: 'I brought them to you, lord, from that wood'. Thereupon, the holy Bishop Colmán said to him: 'A multitude of angels, descending and ascending, often appear to me from that wood as a swarm of bees, which means that a large army of God's family will be there'. At this, the brother said: 'Give me, father, permission to go and stay there'. The holy man replied: 'Go there in peace and, if you are able to live there, I shall also go, so that our resurrection may be there'. The brother found there, however, five monks beginning to work, on seeing whom he returned without delay and told the blessed Bishop Colmán, who said to him: 'This place has been granted by God to them; go brother, therefore, and question their abbot as to whether he will come to me or I to him'. On hearing this, the holy Abbot Mochaomhóg said: 'I shall go to the most distinguished bishop; for I ought to be instructed by his holy standards'. Bishop Colmán was joyful at Mochaomhóg's arrival and lovingly ordered him to bathe, whereupon the blessed abbot bathed himself obediently. Afterwards, as the holy men were conversing with one another, the bishop made a prophecy, saying: 'My brother and co-servant in Christ, this place of mine will frequently be abandoned, so that not even a priest will be able to dwell here because of the battles often fought in this boundary area, whereas your place will always be inhabited and grow larger'. Mochaomhóg replied: 'Father, I shall order that, when this place is deserted, a priest will come from my place in your honour and say mass here'. In fact, there are no more than about four miles between the two places and, having confirmed the fraternity between them and having blessed each other and their places, blessed Mochaomhóg returned with his followers to his place, while the holy bishop remained in his own one. Following this, Mochaomhóg began to build a monastery on his site which grew into the monastic town called Leigh, just as the most blessed prophetess Íde had foretold. As news of most blessed Mochaomhóg's piety spread far and wide, many flocked to him from every side and subjected themselves under him to the yoke of Christ.

16 ~ After that, the aforementioned ruler, who received Mochaomhóg kindly and gave him his place with other gifts, died. Another, by the name of Rónán son of Bleidhín, who arose after him in the kingship, ordered that Mochaomhóg be expelled from his lands and came himself in angry fury with many warriors to expel the holy man of God with violence. But, on descending on the place,

his feet adhered to the ground, and in no way could he move himself from there. Thereupon, when some monks were seen and called over to him, he said: 'Call your holy abbot to me, for behold, a miracle has surely been performed on me because of an evil thought in my heart against the holy man of God'. But the monks said to him: 'He is offering a mass to God just now and afterwards he will be chanting terce, and we dare not tell him before he finishes'. On terce being celebrated, the brethren told the holy man about what had happened to the ruler, but the saint replied: 'Today, I shall not go out until nones have been celebrated'. The ruler remained immobile in this way until noon, when, nones having been sung, Mochaomhóg came to him, to say: 'Tyrant, what benefit do earthly power and cruelty now bring to you, for you came to destroy this place in which you will surely be buried?' The ruler then said to him: 'Servant of God, whatever you say to me, I shall do it, but please release me from this chain'. With that, the saint ordered him to depart and he was released on the spot. Immediately afterwards, in the presence of his chieftains, he granted that place to God, as his predecessor had done, and decreed that he and his family be buried in it. With the holy man then blessing him, he joyfully retired and became very obedient to Mochaomhóg, who loved him greatly.

17 ~ It happened after a time that this same ruler Rónán died and was buried at Mochaomhóg's place, as he had chosen himself. After Rónán's death, however, a certain scribe came to Mochaomhóg's monastery and, on hearing the saint commending the soul of the ruler to God, he reproached the holy man greatly for his commendation of the soul of a man who left this world in the midst of sensual pleasures. The holy man Finnian was then in the monastery of Leigh with other holy men, while that scribe disputed with blessed Mochaomhóg in his presence in a great argument concerning Rónán's soul. Placing many examples before him of divine mercy, Mochaomhóg said: 'Rónán's soul is in God's power, and may He forgive him his sins on my behalf because, as you know, your knowledge is blind and, this being so, your dispute is futile. Also, your death approaches, and your grave will always remain unknown to men, but I shall not excommunicate you, lest you not share in the kingdom of God'. On going away from there, the scribe, becoming separated through the will of God from his folk, died, and his place of burial is unknown to all in accordance with the word of the man of God.

1 Portrait of the Evangelist Mark from the late eighth-century Book of Dimma (TCD, MS A.iv. 23) (image courtesy of the Board of Trinity College Dublin). See also pl. 2.

2 Twelfth-century shrine of the late eighth-century manuscript known as the Book of Dimma. Kept for many centuries in St Crónán's church in Roscrea, the missal and shrine are both now in the library of Trinity College Dublin (MS A.iv. 23). An account is given in Crónán's Life (p. 31) of how the book was completed in the space of forty days and nights, which seemed, miraculously, to the scribe to have been one day only (image courtesy of the Board of Trinity College Dublin).

3 Shrine of the Stowe Missal, made for the abbot of Lorrha between 1026 and 1033 and refurbished in the late fourteenth century. The missal apparently came to be regarded as a relic of St Ruadhán. The shrine is now in the National Museum of Ireland and the missal is in the library of the Royal Irish Academy (image courtesy of the National Museum of Ireland).

4 Roscrea round tower, with high cross in the foreground and remains of the west gable of the medieval church on the right. It was here, according to the saint's Life (p. 38), that Crónán was buried 'with due honour' (© National Monuments Service, Department of the Arts, Heritage and the Gaeltacht).

5 General view of the remains of Monaincha priory. Here, at the 'lake of Cré', Crónán is said to have first settled in the Roscrea area (p. 38) (© National Monuments Service, Department of the Arts, Heritage and the Gaeltacht).

6 Roscrea high cross, with a fully clothed figure of
the crucified Christ. The cross is now housed in the
Black Mills, Roscrea (© National Monuments Service,
Department of the Arts, Heritage and the Gaeltacht).

7 Roscrea round tower and Romanesque doorway (© National Monuments Service, Department of the Arts, Heritage and the Gaeltacht).

8 Beginning of the Life of Crónán in Dublin, Marsh's Library MS Z.3.1.5, fo. 88d (© Marsh's Library, Dublin). Marsh's Library has made the entire manuscript available for educational use as part of the Irish Script On Screen project (www.isos.dias.ie).

9 Remains of Liath (Leigh) Church, which, according to Mochaomhóg's Life (p. 50), took its name from the grey colour of the 'wild and bristly boar' that had previously inhabited the place (© National Monuments Service, Department of the Arts, Heritage and the Gaeltacht).

10 Beginning of the Life of Mochaomhóg of Leigh (*see* pl. 9) in Dublin, Marsh's Library MS Z.3.1.5, fo. 80c (© Marsh's Library, Dublin). Marsh's Library has made the entire manuscript available for educational use as part of the Irish Script On Screen project (www.isos.dias.ie).

11 Remains of the Cistercian abbey of Kilcooly, in the parish of the same name. The abbey was founded in *c.*1182, and it was here, very probably, that Mochaomhóg's Life was written (p. 41) (© National Monuments Service, Department of the Arts, Heritage and the Gaeltacht).

12 Beginning of the Life of Ruadhán of Lorrha in Dublin, Marsh's Library MS Z.3.1.5, fo. 86b (© Marsh's Library, Dublin). Marsh's Library has made the entire manuscript available for educational use as part of the Irish Script On Screen project (www.isos.dias.ie).

13 Remains of the Augustinian priory at Lorrha, founded in the mid-twelfth century. Ruadhán's Life is likely to have been written after the arrival of the Augustinian canons in Lorrha (© National Monuments Service, Department of the Arts, Heritage and the Gaeltacht).

18 ~ After this, Suibhne son of Diarmuid took hold of the chieftaincy of the
kingdom of Éile, while expelling from it Faolán son of Rónán into exile. After
a time, however, when Mochaomhóg had made peace between them, Sléibhín
son of Suibhne treacherously killed by his own hand Faolán son of Rónán,
whom Mochaomhóg had commended on oath to him and his brother. On
hearing of this, holy Mochaomhóg was greatly displeased and went himself
to bear the body to burial. Placing his staff in the ground there, he forgot it
and it grew into a large tree, still there today, and now known, as a sign of the
miracle, by the name of Mochaomhóg. Blessed Abbot Cainneach then also
arrived at the monastery and, as they wished to commit the body together
to the earth, he said to Mochaomhóg: 'You ought not to bury among your
monks this man who was unexpectedly slain'. Mochaomhóg replied: 'I do
not wish to contradict you, father; so let his body be buried apart for a while,
though his soul is in the presence of God in heaven and his place of
resurrection ought thus to be among monks. For the time being, however,
let my staff and chrism be buried with him in an outermost place, and let
them not be released from there until the body of Sléibhín, who disloyally
killed this man, arrives. Also, the hand with which Sléibhín slew him will
quickly fall from his side through God's punishment, and he will die
immediately and be buried here, after which Faolán will come back again to
be buried among the monks'. All was done in this way; Sléibhín, with his
right hand falling from his side, died and, when his body arrived at the
monastery, Faolán's corpse was taken out of the grave and washed in water
and, as all stood around, he came back to life in the presence of the saint.
Then, as Faolán received communion from his hand, Mochaomhóg said:
'Do you wish, my son, to live for a time in this world or depart now for
heaven?' He, however, while giving a clear account of the repose of the just
and of the sufferings of the impious, said to Mochaomhóg: 'My lord father,
the glory of this world is as nothing; let me depart, therefore, quickly to
Christ'. And, with the saint blessing him, he sent forth his spirit, and his body
was buried with due honour among the monks, whereas Sléibhín, his slayer,
was buried outside, where Faolán had first been interred. The ruler Suibhne,
Sléibhín's father, on seeing how God's punishment suddenly came about in
his son, did penance in front of Mochaomhóg, saying: 'Holy lord and master,
shepherd of Christ's faithful, I shall willingly suffer martyrdom or go on a
long pilgrimage, if you should order it, and whatever you say to me, I shall

carry it out, with Christ's help'. On seeing that the ruler was visited by true penance, the man of God said to him: 'Confess your sins and be otherwise faithful in everything, and give alms to the churches of Christ on behalf of your soul and that of your predecessor Rónán, because God is ready to give forgiveness to those who turn to him'. That ruler carried out joyfully what had been ordered to him, and he had a good end to his life in his fort on a certain island in the middle of the River Suir.

19 ~ Once, Fáilbhe Flann, king of the Munstermen, who reigned in the royal fortress of Cashel, ordered his drivers to graze their horses in a field of Mochaomhóg's monastery, where there was much hay. On hearing of this, Mochaomhóg hastened there and, while roughly expelling the horses from his field, treated them badly. When this was announced to the king, he angrily ordered the killing of hostages from the kingdom of Éile, whom he held in chains, unless the ruler of Éile and the parents of the hostages expelled Mochaomhóg from their lands. On learning of this edict, the man of God made his way quickly to the monastic town of Cashel to address the king there and, as they angrily argued with one another, the king said to Mochaomhóg: 'Hairless little one, you will not be given honour here, and you will be expelled from our kingdom'. The holy man replied: 'If I'm hairless, you will be one-eyed'. At these words, intolerably sharp pains began to consume the king's eye, and its sight was extinguished in that way. The king's friends then made many entreaties to the holy man that he might help the king in the name of God, at which the saint said: 'His pains will be prevented, but he will not have sight'. The holy man then blessed water and, on the king washing his eye from it, his pains were relieved, but he was deprived of sight. Yet, the king did not care about this because pains ceased to torment his eye and he slept on the following night.

20 ~ That same night, an extraordinary vision appeared to the king by divine dispensation in which he saw coming in a bright shape a handsome elder who, taking his hand, led him from his seat to the southern wall of the fortress of Cashel. Placed there, he saw the entire plain of Feimhean, which borders on the fortress of Cashel, full of a gathering of holy men, white, distinguished and beautiful in form. When the king questioned the elder as to what this venerable gathering might be, he replied: 'Holy archbishop Patrick, patron of Ireland, and all the saints of Ireland with him, are in that gathering that came to help Mochaomhóg, whom you look down on. I tell you, therefore,

O king, that, unless you should please him, you will die soon and be plunged into the depths of hell'. While the king was still asleep, he saw the elder again take hold of him and, leading him along, place him on the northern wall of the fortress, where a similar vision to the previous one appeared, namely the plain of Mossadh full of most beautiful choirs of people covered in white garments. The fortress of Cashel is positioned on the boundary of two splendid plains, namely Feimhean and Mossadh and, on the king again questioning the elder, the latter said: 'The most glorious virgin Brighid is there, together with holy Íde and all the virgins of Ireland that came to the assistance of Mochaomhóg, whom you unjustly offended. Behold, I preach unto you, O father of this country, that, unless you give him his will, you will perish, and none of your seed will ever reign'. Afterwards, the elder went away from him, the king arose out of his sleep and, when he woke, he told his friends and counsellors what he had seen. They said to him: 'Unless you do what has been ordered to you, your day is done'. With the king sitting in court on the following day, Mochaomhóg was called before him and the king told him in front of the people what the angel had shown him in his dreams. The holy man then gave thanks to God and his saints, and the king humbly carried out Mochaomhóg's will, and, with the saint blessing him, the monarch sent him to his monastery with great honour.

21 ~ At another time, Fáilbhe, king of Cashel, offended Bishop Colmán son of Dáire, Mochaomhóg's friend, whom we mentioned above. Colmán then requested of Mochaomhóg that he accompany him and, going off together, they came to the king, who was in the aforementioned royal town of Cashel, but he, proud in his power and not wishing to agree with the holy men, responded accordingly to them. At this, Mochaomhóg said to him: 'It does not behove you to respond thus to the high bishop who is most holy according to God, and is not lower than you according to the nobility of this world; for you are born of the same race. Two demons, which override you all the time, lord over you, however, namely the demon of pride and the demon of fornication'. The king said: 'In what way can I know if they are dwelling in me?' Mochaomhóg replied: 'You will have signs, for a female whom you love will die this night and two knights will come to you on white horses early tomorrow and converse with you, and you will not know where they come from or go to'. Terrified by what was said, the king then sought forgiveness and piously fulfilled the wish of the holy men and, on they seeing this, blessed Mochaomhóg said to the demon that induced the king's pride: 'Flee, sower

of weeds, from this place and sit on that stone until your associate comes to
you, and I shall speak to you there'. He then expelled the other demon who
incited carnal desire in the king, following which the demons then said to
the holy man: 'Where shall we go?' He replied: 'Go into those two cliffs on
the northern side of this fortress of Cashel, where there is no human access,
and you will harm nobody there until the Day of Judgement'. That place is
dreadful and animals which can climb up there with difficulty are frequently
alarmed, and the crying and muttering of the demons is often heard. On
learning of all of this, the king gave thanks to God and sent the holy men
with honour to their people.

22 ~ On a certain day, Mochaomhóg's monks were working in a wood near the
western part of the monastery, but one of them went apart from the others
and cut down on his own a large tree which, in falling, compressed the
brother's head against another tree. Although, marvellous to say, this did not
break the head, it immobilized the man, who could make no sound. The
brethren then returned home when the hour had come, thinking that the
brother had come with them but, on sitting down to table afterwards, father
Mochaomhóg cast an eye over them and, on failing to see that brother,
questioned them as to where he might be. With all professing not to know,
the holy father said: 'O my little sons, you have forgotten your brother in
great danger'. On saying this, he arose from the table and, with the brethren
following him, set out on a direct route to the place in which the brother was
in torture, but in no way were they able to help him, for, if they were to cut
down the tree, the brother would immediately die. On seeing this great danger,
Mochaomhóg turned to the tree and said: 'I command you in the name of
the Father, Son and Holy Ghost to rise up and stand at your former degree'.
At this, the tree soon arose and stood firmly at its own height, with the sign
of the cut in the timber to be seen for a long time where it stood. The holy
father and his monks, on receiving back their brother unharmed from such
great danger, then gave thanks to God and returned with joy to their church.

23 ~ On another day, when Mochaomhóg's monks were harvesting corn, three of
the brethren died suddenly in the field. On hearing of this, Mochaomhóg set
out quickly, for it displeased him greatly that any of his monks should die a
sudden death. He then blessed water, which, afterwards, by divine influence,
had the force of wine and, when he had besprinkled the dead with the water,
they arose alive, but feeble. On tasting the water, however, they were made

strong, worked with the others, ate, and lived for many a day afterwards. Returning then to his church, Mochaomhóg saw a certain tree full of fruit that was useless to people because of its great sourness; so he blessed the tree with the sign of the cross and all its fruit was turned to sweetness. These three miracles were performed by Mochaomhóg in one day by divine will, namely: wine made from water; dead that were resuscitated; sourness that was changed to sweetness.

24 ~ Two brethren, a young man and an infirm elder, once became ill in Mochaomhóg's monastery and, while the holy father was absent, the young man died and was buried, whereas the elder lived on. On returning and praying to the Lord, Mochaomhóg said: 'In what way did I deserve, my Lord Jesus Christ, to have my young men, whom I want to bring up to serve you, end up dying young, while old infirm men, whose bodily strength deserts them, live on?' Saying this, he ordered the grave to be opened and said to the dead man: 'Rise up, my son, in the name of Jesus Christ'. He rose up immediately, blessing Christ the Saviour of all. Mochaomhóg then asked the aforesaid infirm elder if he wished to depart for Christ, and the old man replied: 'An infirm one ought to covet departing for Christ'. On receiving the sacrament, he happily gave up his spirit, following which an angel of the Lord came to Mochaomhóg, to say: 'Dispose of and adjudge your family as you know and will, servant of Christ, for as long as you live'. By divine influence, Mochaomhóg dispensed this privilege, given to him by God, to his people.

25 ~ On a certain appointed day, most blessed Abbot Cainneach promised to come to Mochaomhóg at Leigh on the ninth hour but, having forgotten this promise, he remained until noon on that day in his own monastery, namely Aghaboe in the kingdom of Ossory. Then, on remembering, he heaved a sigh to God because he had not fulfilled what he promised to the holy man and, inspired by God's dispensation, he began to run, and moved so quickly that he sang with Mochaomhóg on the same ninth hour in the monastery of Leigh. Only God himself, who led him most quickly, knows what happened in that matter, because he concealed from him and from us everything except what he might have traversed through his own powers; a journey between these two monasteries, Leigh and Aghaboe, lasts a full day for most pedestrians. Mochaomhóg ordered that a bath be prepared, and said to Cainneach: 'Sing a mass for us, father, in the meantime, until the brethren return from duty', but Cainneach was not willing. When seated afterwards at table in the

refectory, however, blessed Cainneach cut off a piece of bread from which the brethren saw a stream of blood running into the ground. Mochaomhóg then said softly to him: 'Lord father, let us return to the church, and let you offer God a sacrifice of praise, for my brethren and I greatly desire this'. The blessed elder Cainneach then sang a mass for God, as Mochaomhóg desired and, when the holy men returned after the sacrifice, they saw the bread fresh and without a cut. At this, they gave thanks to the Lord Jesus Christ and ate with spiritual enjoyment.

26 ~ At another time, some brethren came to the monastery of Leigh, wishing to see Mochaomhóg and talk to him. At that time, Mochaomhóg was working in a field near the monastery with his brethren and, when the visitors enquired as to which he might be, the saint was pointed out to them on his knees working, at which they were amazed. On being addressed by them, however, Mochaomhóg made a prophecy, saying: 'Brethren, think of the healing of your souls; death is approaching and soon all of you will die, except that little boy with you'. They, not doubting the prophecy, did penance, and were dead after a few days. They were five in number, and Mochaomhóg kept the little boy with him and taught him. He became the holy Abbot Daghán who is buried in the monastery of Ennereilly, on the lands of the Dál Meisin Corb in the territory of the Leinstermen, in the eastern part of Ireland. And another boy studied with Daghán under the most blessed father Mochaomhóg.

27 ~ On a certain day, holy father Mochaomhóg said to blessed Daghán: 'My son, if you study well, you will receive communion of the body and blood of Christ from my hand before you die'. After a few days, however, that holy boy was killed. The people of Ossory came to lay waste the kingdom of Éile on a day on which Daghán was minding the calves of the monastery's cows with his companion, and all others were busy at their different tasks; so, on coming across the pious cowherds, the warriors of the ruler of Ossory cut off Daghán's head, while the other escaped with his throat cut. Cainneach was then in the monastery of Leigh and, when the one who escaped with a cut throat came to him and Mochaomhóg, together with their brethren, the grace of God restored the youth to health there through His holy men. Daghán's body, however, including its trunk, was brought back to the monastery together with its head. Mochaomhóg then said to Cainneach: 'I promised this youth, holy father, to give him divine communion before death but, as I have not carried it out, let divine power be magnified in him through us, and let you

join, father, the head to the body and ask God to revive him'. Cainneach
replied: 'I shall join the head to the body in the name of Christ, whereas you
may ask God to restore his soul to him'. Then, taking hold of the head, the
blessed elder Cainneach joined it firmly to the body as it was before, but
a circular scar remained about the throat until his death; then, with
Mochaomhóg praying and Cainneach still holding Daghán in his hands, the
most fortunate youth rose up alive and well to the saints, while blessing the
Lord. Having received communion from Mochaomhóg's hands, as was
promised to him, Daghán, whose life was renowned for miracles, lived for a
long time afterwards, and he stood out as the father of monks in his previously
mentioned place.

28 ~ At a certain time, Colmán son of Fearadhach, ruler of Ossory, thinking that
an enemy of his, Fíonán by name, had fled before him to Mochaomhóg's
monastery in order to hide there, came and searched every building for that
wretched one. Mochaomhóg said to the ruler: 'I sought three petitions from
God against you, of which two were denied, but the third was conceded. The
first petition was that you would die soon, but God granted to holy Fachtna
that you should live for another fourteen years; the second was that you
should not reside in heaven but, on Cainneach's account, it will be allowed
to you to dwell there; the third, then, which was granted by God, was that
you would be separated from your kingship before the end of the month'. On
hearing these words, the king did penance and brought gifts to God and to
holy Mochaomhóg, who now said to him: 'You will be removed from your
authority and barely escape the danger of death but, because you have some
holy men as friends, you will reign in all your power after three days. My
friend, the holy elder Cainneach, will help you in all things'. After this, the
ruler, rejoicing at such a prophecy, went away with a blessing.

29 ~ Mochaomhóg commended a certain church to his disciple Mochoime and
the latter first erected there a church-building and refectory. In the meantime,
Mochaomhóg, Cainneach, Molua son of Oiche, and Mofheaca came together
one night in that place, and there was no roofed house except the church-
building. Mochaomhóg's disciple, the superior of the place, then said: 'You
go into the church-building, because we do not have another house ready'.
But Mofheaca, who is also called Féichín, said to him: 'No, but we will go
into the refectory, for, although roofless, our God will not let wind or rain
descend on us this night'. With the holy men eating in the roofless refectory,

and remaining afterwards in it, Molua said: 'There will always be an abundance of riches in the place in which this generous supper was given to us'. Mochaomhóg then said: 'This roofless upright building of mine, under which God will protect us from wind and rain on this tempestuous night, will be blessed, and an illustrious building will not be lacking here for all time'. Cainneach said: 'A son of death will not die in this place'. In this way, the holy men gave a blessing to the place, and their blessing will never be lacking there. As the fathers were going away, the pious disciple Mochoime, master of the place, said to them: 'Are you leaving me here alone, holy men of God?' The men replied: 'We shall be with you here in spirit, and you will be the holy man here and meet up with us on God's Judgement Day, for which you will have this sign'. With that, the men of God placed five small stones in the burial ground, which, as a sign of their promise, remain unmoved to this day through their grace, and nobody can move them from there.

30 ~ At another time, a magnate of the Uí Aonghusa, of the people of the Déise to whom, as we said above, Mochaomhóg's mother belonged, and another magnate of that people by the name of Faolán son of Eacha, who were enemies of one another, swore a peace between them in Mochaomhóg's presence, each taking the other in a pledge from the hand of the holy man. Afterwards, the magnate of the Uí Aonghusa, breaking his pledge, killed Faolán son of Eacha; and holy father Mochaomhóg, on hearing of this, came in great anger to curse him or call him to penance, but the heart of that man was hardened, and he said: 'I don't mind if you do something, Mochaomhóg, because most holy Cuimín Fada son of Fiachna blessed me diligently and promised me the kingdom of heaven and earth'. On hearing these sentences, Mochaomhóg said: 'Whom Cuimín blessed, I shall not curse, but I shall curse your wife and son'. But that lady then came with her son to Mochaomhóg and, bending her knees before him, said: 'Spare us, lord, in the name of Christ, and whatever you will say to us, we shall willingly do because, as you know, lord father, we cannot chastise our master, who offended you'. Though accepting satisfaction from them, Mochaomhóg said: 'I shall curse that lake which surrounds him and is a great protection'. For the very secure fortress of that magnate was in the middle of a deep lake and, on the holy man cursing the lake, it appeared immediately as land, with no one knowing where the water had retreated to. Up to this, the magnate persevered in the hardness of his heart, but then the holy man said: 'I shall curse your daughter, whom you love greatly, and your strongest and swiftest horse, which you rely on in battles'; and, on his cursing

them, they immediately died. When the magnate saw this, he did penance at heart and made satisfaction, while appealing in the name of Christ for his lake, daughter and horse. The holy man then said: 'All things are possible to our Lord God, but I shall pray for the will of Christ to be done in them'. When Mochaomhóg had prayed, the lake was filled immediately with its water, as it had been before, and the daughter was restored to life, and the strong and swift horse lived once more. When he saw this, the magnate granted a site on which to build a church to God and Mochaomhóg who, having imposed a penance, and having put that church in order, returned to his monastery, while giving thanks to God.

31 ~ Bishop Fursa and most blessed Abbot Mochaomhóg loved greatly a youth who was called a pupil of theirs because he used to live frequently with them from boyhood onwards; the holy men used to teach and foster him in true religion and honesty of life. The chieftain Cuán fettered that youth, namely Scanlán son of Faolán of noble race, and placed him in custody, because he feared him greatly as the youth ought to be chieftain, as he was. On hearing of this, the holy men, Fursa and Mochaomhóg, made their way to entreat the chieftain Cuán on behalf of their beloved Scanlán; Mochaomhóg said to him: 'Lord chieftain, hand over our friend to us unharmed, for he is innocent towards you'. But the chieftain replied: 'In truth, up to now he did me no evil, but I'm afraid that he will do so, by competing with me for the chieftaincy'. Mochaomhóg replied: 'I promise that he will not harm you during your lifetime'. Having been calmed by this, the chieftain said: 'I shall do what you wish, but come with me to the town of Cashel, and I shall hand him over in front of the king so that he may be a witness'. On arriving there, he gave them the youth Scanlán in the presence of the king, and they departed peacefully from one another. When Mochaomhóg had appealed to the chieftain Cuán on behalf of the youth Scanlán, the archbishop of the monastic town of Emly was staying with the king in the town of Cashel, and said prophetically to him: 'Lord king, are you fond of your chieftain Cuán?' The king replied: 'Indeed, I am'. The bishop then said: 'Send word to him quickly, therefore, that he give Mochaomhóg his pleasure; for whatever day on which he will have displeased him, he will die'. This, then, was fulfilled afterwards because, with the chieftain Cuán again offending Mochaomhóg, and the saint seeking divine assistance against him, he died immediately and, through Mochaomhóg's grace, Scanlán son of Faolán, pupil of the holy men, was ordained chieftain of his territory by the king. The king then said to the

aforementioned bishop: 'What merit do you think Mochaomhóg has?' The bishop replied: 'I know this truly; if Mochaomhóg were to say to the mountain of Cua that it cross the River Suir in place of the plain of Feimhean, and that the plain leave its site for it, the Lord would do all of that in his honour'. Giving thanks, the king then blessed the Lord.

32 ~ A certain good man named Díoma, a son of Féichín, was a faithful friend of Mochaomhóg. He requested of the saint in the name of the Holy Trinity that, should he fall ill at some stage, the holy man would deign to come to him so that he might receive the Lord's communion from his hand at the hour of death. The man of God promised him this and, after a long time, Díoma, now in poor health, sent a messenger to Mochaomhóg that he might come to him, but the holy man was then staying in the monastery called Inishlounaght, in the southern part of the territory of Ossory, near the estuary of the sea into which the River Nore flows. On hearing that, Mochaomhóg hurriedly went on his way, but before he could come, his friend Díoma died and there was great mourning over him, though he was not yet buried when the saint arrived. Mochaomhóg watched over the body that night with others until midnight. The holy man then took a burning torch, approached the bier alone and, making the sign of the holy cross over the body, said: 'My dear friend, Díoma, arise in the name of Christ and accept the divine last sacrament from my hand, as your faith obtained'. At these words, Díoma, blessing God, arose as if from a heavy sleep, and the holy man said to him: 'Which will please you now; to live again with yours or to return to the repose you witnessed?' On hearing this conversation, those who were in the house gathered around and, when they saw their lord alive, gave thanks to God. With him, however, electing and praying to depart from this world, Mochaomhóg gave him communion in front of all. He then offered his seed after him to be always buried near Mochaomhóg, before falling asleep again in peace, and Mochaomhóg with his people buried the corpse in his monastery of Leigh.

33 ~ Once, most blessed Abbot Mochaomhóg sent one of his monks to the western part of Ireland who, as he was returning, died in the monastic town of Emly in the plain of Munster, and was buried there. The monk was called Cuán Cearr and Mochaomhóg, when he heard the news, went off to bring the body back to his monastery. But the archbishop of that monastic town did not surrender to him the body of the monk and, while they were disputing,

Mochaomhóg said to the pontiff: 'Do you regard it as just that you retain the body of a monk who offered his body and soul to God in my monastery?' The pontiff replied: 'Not I but God knows'. On hearing this, Mochaomhóg said to him: 'So that you may know that you are doing wrong, lord bishop, you will witness Christ's power in him'. As Mochaomhóg reached the grave of his monk, it was opened by God in front of him and, when the holy father took hold of his brother's hand, he arose from the grave with him. The bishop, glorifying Christ in a loud voice, then said to all: 'I ought not to retain a living monk, whom my God raised from the dead according to the manner of Lazarus, through the merits of his servant, and God knows that I did not do so out of malice, but in order to have holy remains in the cemetery of this church'. Afterwards, having received the permission and blessing of the prelate, Mochaomhóg and his monk Cuán Cearr returned to their monastery rejoicing in Christ, and this Cuán Cearr afterwards built at the behest of his master the monastery called Clashmore, and dwelt there in great sanctity for many a day until he departed for Christ after a happy end.

34 ~ Through some occurrence, a consecrated virgin named Cainnear lost the light of her eyes and was blind for a long time. Having been brought to Mochaomhóg, she appealed to him in the name of Christ to bless her eyes, and the man of God did so; then, having consecrated water, he commanded her to wash her face in it. On the holy virgin washing her face in the water, she regained her sight there in the presence of all. Again seeing both heaven and earth, she returned to her own church in which, joyful at heart, she blessed God in his miracles through his holy servants.

35 ~ After our patron, most blessed Mochaomhóg, gave back as a gift the light of this world, God called him to eternal light, to cohabit with the saints. Now weakened, he blessed both the brethren and his churches and, in the presence of an assembled multitude of saints, he most joyfully gave back his holy soul to God on 13 March. He was then buried with due honour in his holy monastery of Leigh, where many miracles are performed through him by Christ. His is honour and glory with God the Father and the Holy Ghost forever and ever. Amen.

Thus ends the Life of Holy Mochaomhóg, abbot and confessor.

The Life of Ruadhán of Lorrha

THE SAINT

Aonghas of Tallaght, the early ninth-century martyrologist, was obliged by his choice of metre to be sparing in his praise of individual saints, to whom he usually gave no more than two of the four lines allowed by it. Arriving at 12 September, for example, he accounted for Ailbhe, Munster's premier saint, with a brief exhortation that the feast be celebrated with a 'luminous and flowing repast'.[1] His treatment of Ruadhán at 15 April was of a different order. Devoting an entire quatrain to him, he used three metaphors, *prímdae breó* (pre-eminent flame), *lie lógmar* (precious stone) and *lócharn* (lamp), to demonstrate his high regard for the saint.[2] Given the closeness of the connection between Lorrha and Tallaght, both of which were prominent *céili Dé* churches, Aonghas's decision to eulogize Ruadhán in this manner was a natural one.[3] Both churches are also brought together in a poem preserved in the margins of the Book of Leinster version of the Martyrology of Tallaght that associates their patronal days with the activities of Ireland's birds.[4]

Among many other measures of Ruadhán's standing was his selection as one of those considered comparable to an apostle, in his case Matthias, the man chosen to replace Judas.[5] He was also numbered among Ireland's own apostles – otherwise some noted pupils of Finnian of Clonard, whose famous school he reputedly attended (§1). His place in the surviving Munster versions of the corpus of saints' pedigrees is also indicative of his high rank. In the earliest of these, the no-longer-extant eleventh-century Psalter of Cashel, whose version of the corpus is now known only from a list of contents drawn

---

1 *MartO* 194; Stokes erroneously took the Irish *fleid*, 'feast, repast', to be the name of another saint, thus reducing his praise of Ailbhe to a single line.   2 The quatrain reads: *Prímdae breó nád athbi/arfich tola tothlai/ba cain lie lógmar/Ródán lócharn Lothrai* (A pre-eminent flame that is unebbing, that vanquishes illicit desires, fair was the precious stone, Ruadhán, the lamp of Lothra); the text as in Stokes' edition (*MartO* 106), with slight modification of the translation.   3 On the other hand, while Ruadhán was invoked well down the list of native saints in the Stowe Missal's first litany, Ailbhe was placed second after Patrick and, of the two, only Ailbhe appears in the second litany (Plummer, *Irish litanies*, 14). 4 *MartT* 94.   5 Ó Riain, *Corpus*, §712.14; ibid., §208.

up in June 1619, the 'pedigrees of our principall saincts' leads off with the three national saints (Patrick, Brighid and Colum Cille), followed by Ailbhe, Ruadhán and Déaglán.[6] The version of the corpus drawn up in Lorrha itself in the third quarter of the fourteenth century, while omitting Ailbhe entirely and ceding first place to Patrick, gave Ruadhán the honour of second place, followed by Molua, patron of the diocese of Killaloe, Brighid, Flannán (co-patron of Killaloe), Crónán of Roscrea, Ciarán of Seirkieran and Odhrán of Latteragh.[7] In the same text, Ruadhán's pedigree is traced over two folios to Adam 'son of God on earth', a distinction given to no other Irish saint.[8]

Ruadhán's status is further emphasized by his mention in several twelfth-century sources, including the Life of Fionnbharr of Cork, which brings disciples of the Lorrha saint to a church named Ceall na Cluaine.[9] Although relatively obscure, this church appears to have been patronized by the MacCarthys following their expulsion from Cork by the Anglo-Normans, thus rendering it worthy of the considerable honour of being chosen as the place in which Fionnbharr died.[10] Ruadhán's cult became established at Aghinagh, not far from Ceall na Cluaine, and among other churches dedicated to him in south Munster were Templeroan near Doneraile, Kilruane near Glanmire, Kilroan near Kinsale, and Kilruane near Ross Carbery.[11]

Ruadhán's adoption as patron by the MacCarthys also appears to underlie an episode in the Vision of Tnúthghal, a text compiled in Germany about 1150 by Marcus of the Regensburg Schottenkloster, whose community was largely made up of natives of Munster.[12] Marcus gave Ruadhán the privilege of being one of the occupants of the heavenly *campus laetitiae*, 'plain of happiness', as witnessed by Tnúthghal – supposedly a knight of Cormac Mac Carthaigh – who described the saint as his *patronus*. The saint's standing among the monks of the Regensburg Schottenkloster may also be reflected in an image on a wall near the entrance to their church, which shows a figure named 'Rydan' holding keys.[13] A note added to the *Kilkenniensis* version of the saint's Life states that his arm was kept as a relic in Canterbury, but this is more likely to refer to Rónán of Dromiskin.[14] Among his relics, however, was a bell bearing his name, now in the British Museum, London.[15]

How Ruadhán was viewed in Lorrha itself will be made clear by the discussion that follows of the Life written for him there. In advance of this,

6 Ó Riain, 'The Psalter', 122.   7 Ó Riain, *Corpus*, xxxv.   8 Ó Riain, *Corpus*, §208.   9 Ó Riain, *Beatha Bharra*, 70–2 §§26–7.   10 Ó Riain, *The making of a saint*, 115–16.   11 *DIS* 543.   12 Pfeil, *Die Vision*, 24–5.   13 Ó Riain-Raedel, 'Cashel and Germany', 189.   14 *VSHP* ii, 242n.   15 Stokes and Petrie, *Christian inscriptions*, ii, 94.

9 The door-keeper inside the former Schottenkloster (Irish monastery) in Regensburg, Germany. The figure, named Rydan, may represent Ruadhán (image courtesy of Diarmuid Ó Riain).

however, the summary of the saint's virtues in the Life's final chapter may be quoted as a measure of the view from Lorrha:

> Now, since he was born of a race of kings, father Ruadhán had a regal form, the length of his body being twelve feet; externally handsome and more beautiful internally; he was noble according to men, more noble according to God; great in body, but even greater in grace; large in front of men, but even larger in front of God; full of love and humility, patience, mercy, and other good works. For all of these good things, our patron Ruadhán received great glory from God and men.

THE CHURCH

As Patrick was leaving Munster, he came, according to the author of the tripartite Life, to the kingdom of Múscraighe Tíre (later the Tipperary baronies of Upper Ormond and Lower Ormond), where he was met by three brothers, 'powerful in that region'.[16] The first of the brothers to believe was Muinneach, whom the saint baptized and blessed, promising to his issue the 'high kingship'

---

16 Mulchrone, *Bethu Phátraic*, 2460–5 (= Stokes, *The tripartite Life*, 210). Cf. O'Brien, *Corpus*, 323f51.

of the kingdom forever. The king met by the mid-ninth-century Armagh clerics, who prepared the ground for Patrick's quite unhistorical journey in Munster, was probably Dúnghalach son of Seachnasach, descendant of Muinneach and eponym of the family of Uí Dhúnghalaigh, who retained the kingship of Múscraighe Tíre, not 'forever' but at least until the end of the eleventh century: Dúnghalach's son Ciarán was slain 'by his own people' in 898, and Fionn Ua Dúnghalaigh, *rídhamhna* of Múscraighe Tíre, the last of his family to be named in the genealogies, died in a 'great pestilence' in 1095.[17] By then, in the wake of Dál gCais expansion, the Uí Cheinnéidigh had already been intruded into the kingship of Múscraighe, as is shown by an entry in the Annals of Inisfallen for 1037, which notes the killing of Cú Choille son of Ceinnéidigh, king of Múscraighe, 'in front of the stone church of Lorrha', which was probably a monument to the Dál gCais presence in the area.[18] At this point, Dál gCais abbots had also begun to be intruded into the coarbship at Lorrha. By the end of the twelfth century, however, the Uí Cheinnéidigh had been displaced in their turn by Anglo-Norman adventurers.

Lorrha is not mentioned in the tripartite Life, which dates to about the middle of the ninth century, but already then it was probably the chief church of Múscraighe Tíre.[19] It also had custody of what must have been a substantial shrine of its patron Ruadhán because an incursion into north Tipperary by Vikings about this time resulted in its breaking.[20] Lorrha appears also to have come to prominence during this period as a church associated with the *céili Dé*; it was here, for example, that the Stowe Missal, one of the more important productions of this group, was kept, perhaps together with the Martyrology of Tallaght, and possibly from a date soon after these two texts were compiled in the early ninth century.[21] To mark Lorrha's custody of the Stowe Missal, a shrine, now in the National Museum of Ireland (Dublin), was commissioned for it in the early eleventh century by Ruadhán's coarb, Mathghamhain Ua Cathail (d. 1037), and the work this involved was sponsored by Fionn Ua Dúnghalaigh, then king of Múscraighe Tíre (d. 1033).[22]

By the mid-twelfth century, Lorrha had been chosen as the location of a priory of canons regular of St Augustine, a development that underlines its continuing importance; the canons usually placed their foundations in or near ecclesiastical centres of high standing.[23] About this time, however, or soon

---

17 *AI* 1095.13; O'Brien, *Corpus*, 323f6. **18** Ó Carragáin, 'Patterns of patronage', 30–1. **19** See Gwynn and Gleeson, *A history*, 48: obits of twelve of its abbots are noted for the period 700–1107. **20** Todd, *Cogadh Gaedhel re Gallaibh*, 16 §17. **21** Ó Riain, *Feastdays*, 115, 118; Gwynn and Gleeson, *A history*, 49–52; O'Rahilly, 'The history'. **22** Ó Riain, 'The shrine', 285–95. **23** Gwynn and Hadcock, *Medieval*

afterwards, in 1154, 1157 and 1179, the site was among several in the south of Ireland to be burned by unidentified parties.[24] This was probably as a result of the anarchic conditions that gave twelfth-century Ireland a character of 'peculiar chaos'.[25] By the 1150s, the canons regular had a network of priories throughout Ireland. Furthermore, the order appears to have played a central role in promoting interest in the native Irish saints. The canons were certainly involved in the production of almost every known martyrology from this period, possibly beginning with the Book of Leinster version of the Martyrology of Tallaght, whose exemplar may have come from Lorrha.[26]

In addition to their involvement in the production of martyrologies, the canons regular had a keen eye for the benefits to be drawn from traditional practices of pilgrimage, gaining charge of some of the more important centres. Skellig Michael, for example, off the coast of Kerry, was served by an Augustinian priory at Ballinskelligs on the mainland.[27] Pilgrimage to Patrick's Purgatory on Lough Derg was likewise put on a firm footing by the canons of Armagh, who established a dependency on Saints' Island, possibly as early as the 1130s.[28] There was, of course, a material basis for the promotion of pilgrimage to sites associated with saints; pilgrims were a valuable source of the revenue needed to sustain priories and, though no record survives of pilgrimage to Lorrha, the preservation there of such relics as the arm of Ruadhán in a silver case would indicate that the saint's cult was actively promoted by the canons, no doubt especially about the time of his annual commemoration on 15 April.[29] This is also shown by the previously mentioned shrine of the Stowe Missal, which was fashioned between 1026 and 1033, no doubt for display purposes. By then, the missal was probably already regarded as a relic of Ruadhán.

During the thirteenth century, when the pre-Conquest rulers of Múscraighe Tíre, the Uí Cheinnéidigh, had made way for Anglo-Norman adventurers, some lands appear to have fallen to Walter de Burgo, earl of Ulster, who founded a Dominican friary at Lorrha in 1269.[30] Little notice is taken of the place from then onwards, however, either in the annals, which almost totally ignore it, or in other records. During the period of native Irish revival in the fourteenth century, its Augustinian priory appears nevertheless to have commanded resources sufficient for the refurbishment of the shrine of its

religious houses, 185.   **24** *AFM s.a.*   **25** Byrne, *Irish kings and high-kings*, 269.   **26** Ó Riain, *Feastdays*, 115.   **27** Gwynn and Hadcock, *Medieval religious houses*, 192.   **28** Ibid., 193.   **29** *MartO* 116; *MartT* 33. **30** Gwynn and Hadcock, *Medieval religious houses*, 227.

10 Figure over the door at the Augustinian priory at Lorrha, founded in the mid-twelfth century (image © National Monuments Service, Department of the Arts, Heritage and the Gaeltacht).

missal, which was undertaken at the behest of Giolla Ruadháin Ó Macáin, Ruadhán's coarb, some time before his death in 1381.[31] Giolla Ruadháin was a cultivated man; he also commissioned a manuscript consisting mainly of genealogies and king lists, many of them of local importance. Among other features of this manuscript is its previously mentioned collection of saints' genealogies which places Ruadhán second after Patrick and traces the saint's pedigree to Adam.[32]

THE LIFE

Lives of saints provided a means of protecting and promoting the interests of the new orders which began to arrive in Ireland in the second quarter of the twelfth century. As I have argued elsewhere, the biography composed for Ruadhán – which has survived in Latin and Irish versions – belongs in this category.[33] This is despite the fact that one Latin version forms part of a group of Lives in the Salamancan codex, known as the O'Donohue Lives, whose constituent texts are sometimes taken to date to as early as the period 750–850.[34] A critical edition of Ruadhán's entire biographical dossier has yet to be undertaken but, as in other Lives belonging to this group, there are many indications in the Life of Ruadhán of a date after the arrival in Lorrha of the canons regular of St Augustine.

As already remarked, Ruadhán was described by the genealogists as a son of Fearghas Bearn of the Síol Duach (alias Uí Dhuach of Airgeadros) in Ossory, whose lands are now represented by the Kilkenny baronies of Fassadinin and Crannagh.[35] The saint's biographer adhered to this tradition (§1), and also gave it practical application by locating one episode in Tullaroan (Tulach Ruadháin) in the present barony of Crannagh, a site named from the saint (§28). Although there is no reference to the saint's mother in the Life, his two sisters, Caol and Ruadhnaid, receive mention (§15), and Caol, mother of 'Ruadhán the priest', is among the entries in a tract on the mothers of the saints.[36]

Following his birth among the Uí Dhuach of Ossory, Ruadhán is brought for his education to Finnian of Clonard, after which he founded his first church

31 Ó Riain, 'The shrine', 285–95.   32 Ó Riain, *Corpus*, xxxv.   33 Ó Riain, 'The O'Donohue Lives', 48–9; cf. Ó Riain, 'Fíonán of Iveragh'.   34 Sharpe, *Medieval Irish saints' Lives*, 297–339.   35 *ATigIndex* 192; Ó Riain, Ó Murchadha and Murray, *Historical dictionary*, i, 46.   36 Ó Riain, *Corpus*, §722.44. A separate text includes him, with many other unlikely siblings, among the saints said to have been children

in Múscraighe Tíre – probably at Kilruane (Ceall Ruadháin) in Lower Ormond
– thus establishing an immediate connection with the kingdom that was to
support his main foundation (§1).[37] He soon moved from there, however, on
angelic advice to where his *civitas*, now Lorrha, was located (§2). The site
chosen at Lorrha was allegedly the lair of a wild boar, a topos frequently used
with a view to emphasizing the sacred nature of a site (§3). At this point, the
saint's presence in Lorrha is said to have disturbed Bréanainn – at a nearby
location called Tulach Bhréanainn – who then moved to the site of his own
principal church at Clonfert (§4). Ruadhán's wider wanderings then began,
first to Ulster, where he settled at Slanore (Snámh Luthair) in the Cavan parish
of Kilmore, and at 'Ros Énni', apparently in Co. Armagh (§§7, 8).

From Ulster, Ruadhán arrived in Connacht – among the Uí Oilealla who
gave name to the Sligo barony of Tirerrill – to visit an otherwise unrecorded
'sister', Dairí by name, founding there the church of Shancough (§9). Close
by, in the Roscommon parish of Tibohine, is Kilrooan (Ceall Ruadháin),
which probably takes its name from the saint.

Returning to Munster, Ruadhán is shown performing various strategically
well-placed acts, most of them miraculous. These included: the blessing of
the hands of a youth in Araidh Chliach, the area about Emly, historically
Munster's chief church (§11); the restoration to health of the wife of the king
of Cuala, near Dublin (§12); the raising, at the request of Bréanainn, from
the bottom of the Shannon Estuary of a sunken boat and its valuable passenger,
the son of the king of the Britons, whom he protected from drowning (§13).
Subsequently, the saint is given the opportunity of showing deference to his
former teacher, Finnian of Clonard, by acceding to the latter's request that
the community at Lorrha desist from receiving all the sustenance they needed
from the sap of a miraculous tree (§14). There followed the 'Cursing of Tara'
episode (§§15–18), the only one in the Life to have attracted much attention.[38]
In it, the king of Tara, having offended Ruadhán by taking prisoner a fugitive
under the saint's protection, engaged with the holy man in a litany of curses,
including the prediction (often cited by later poets) that Tara would become
desolate. Various other miracles are then performed, including one while the
saint was residing at Derrynaflan (Doire Eidhneach) (§25), and another

---

of Inghean Bhaoith of Killinaboy (Grosjean, 'Poems on St Senan', 93–5). **37** Cf. Gwynn and Gleeson,
A history, 47. **38** Ruadhán's penchant for cursing has caught the attention of historians; all six references
to Ruadhán in Byrne, *Irish kings and high-kings*, relate to this episode, and the saint's 'love of cursing' is
singled out in Ó Cróinín, *Early medieval Ireland*.

involving the restoration to life of a number of kings at Tullaroan (§28).[39] The
concluding chapters (§§29–30) present the saint as overcoming, together with
Colum Cille, a host of demons at Rahugh near Durrow, the church of Aodh
son of Breac, before going on to list Ruadhán's many virtues.

The itinerary thus drawn up for the saint takes him, literally, all over the
country, often to places named after him. Throughout his journey Ruadhán
is seldom allowed, however, to stray far from a priory connected with the
canons regular of St Augustine. Finnian, Ruadhán's tutor, who is shown great
deference, was patron of Clonard, one of the earliest and most important of
the Augustinian houses in Ireland.[40] Like Finnian, Bréanainn was patron of a
church (Clonfert) that became the site of a house of Augustinian canons about
the same time as Lorrha, and this coincidence may underlie the claim in the
text that Bréanainn, having been disturbed by Ruadhán's arrival in Lorrha,
went off to found Clonfert (§4).[41] Ruadhán's intervention on this saint's behalf
in the Shannon Estuary, by saving from drowning a son of the king of the
Britons, would have been sure to impress, especially after the English conquest
of Ireland. Furthermore, it is scarcely a coincidence that Bréanainn's (only)
foundation in this area, at Canon Island, took its name from the Augustinian
canons.[42]

Closely related to the canons regular were the Premonstratensian canons
whose priory on Lough Key included Shancough – the church allegedly
founded by Ruadhán – among its possessions.[43] Lough Key was also the
mother-house of the priory of Lough Oughter in Cavan, located within a few
hundred yards of the church of Slanore, which was supposedly visited by the
Lorrha saint.[44] Finally, Pollrone (Poll Ruadháin), the location of the celebrated
'Cursing of Tara' episode, formed part of the possessions of the neighbouring
convent of Kilculliheen, a house of Augustinian canonesses founded by
Diarmuid Mac Murrough in 1151.[45] Clearly, then, a substantial part of the
Life of Ruadhán is most easily explained by reference to Lorrha's position
within the countrywide network of houses of Augustinian canons, thus
pointing to an earliest possible date for the composition of the text in the
second quarter of the twelfth century, when these priories began to be founded.

---

39 The Tullaroan location for this episode is supported by the mention of a place called 'Cuillinn'.
Historically, the church of Tullaroan was attached to the head-church of Callainn, now Callan in Co.
Kilkenny.   40 Gwynn and Hadcock, *Medieval religious houses*, 163–4.   41 Ibid., 164–5.   42 Ibid.,
162; *DIS* 116.   43 Gwynn and Hadcock, *Medieval religious houses*, 205; Freeman, *The Compossicion
Booke*, 129, 154.   44 Gwynn and Hadcock, *Medieval religious houses*, 206.   45 Ibid., 319–20.

MANUSCRIPTS AND PREVIOUS EDITIONS

The Latin Life has been preserved in the Marsh's Library, Dublin, MS Z.3.1.5 (M, *Kilkenniensis*), Trinity College Dublin, MS E.iii.11 (T), Bibliothèque Royale, Brussels, MS 7672–4 (S, *Salmanticensis*), and Bodleian Library, Oxford, MSS Rawlinson B485 (R) and B505 collections. The Irish Life is preserved in Bibliothèque Royale, Brussels, MS 2324–40 (Br), and Royal Irish Academy, Dublin, MS A iv 1. The Salamancan version has been edited in *Acta sanctorum* (Apr. ii, 382–6), then in De Smedt and De Backer, *Acta sanctorum Hiberniae*, cols 319–32, and again by W.W. Heist in *VSHH* 160–7. The Irish version was edited and translated by Charles Plummer in *BNÉ* i, 317–29; ii, 308–20. The present translation is based on the Latin text preserved in M and T, as edited by Charles Plummer in *VSHP* ii, 240–52, collated with S (as edited by Heist), R and Br.

The Life of Saint Ruadhán, abbot of Lorrha

Here begins the Life of Ruadhán, abbot and confessor

1 ~ The most blessed Abbot Ruadhán was born of the most noble family of Ireland, the people of Eoghanacht. His father Byrra belonged to the seed of Duach, and, as we said, was of the people of Eoghanacht, but lived in Ossory in the western part of Leinster. His family, which still lives in the same region, is now known as Uí Dhuach. Already in his mother's womb, Ruadhán was one of God's elect; from infancy onwards, he loved God with all his heart and, from youth onwards, miracles began to happen through him. Inspired by the Holy Spirit, he then left his parents and home-place and went off to Finnian, a most learned man who lived in the monastic town of Clonard on the border between Leinster and the kingdom of Meath. Blessed Ruadhán remained there with the aforesaid Finnian, reading the various scriptures and making great progress in them; the blessedness of holy Ruadhán's life allowed mastery in many subjects.

When blessed Ruadhán had become learned in all disciplines, his master Finnian made him receive priestly orders. When he had received these, the abbot sent him with some monks to his own province of Munster so that he might build there a place for God. Bidding his master farewell, blessed Ruadhán came with his disciples into the province of Munster, and entered the territory of Múscraighe Tíre, in which, having discovered a site, he began to build a monastery for God.

2 ~ When Ruadhán had remained in great holiness in that place for some time, an angel of the Lord came to him, to say: 'Your resurrection will not be in this church, servant of God, but you will rise again at the coming of Christ in the place called Lorrha'. In compliance with the word of the angel, Ruadhán then put his church in order, and went from there to the place of his resurrection.

3 ~ On Ruadhán's arrival at the aforesaid place, a wild boar, fearful of him, abandoned its hollow, for that place in the above-mentioned kingdom of Múscraighe was deserted before holy father Ruadhán founded the great

monastery of Lorrha, in which he himself is buried. A great monastic town of the same name grew up there, and Ruadhán led an admirable life in it, with God performing many miracles through him while he was alive, and his grace is still much in evidence.

4 ~ Holy Abbot Bréanainn built a church, called in Irish Tulach Bhréanainn, that is Bréanainn's Hill, not far from Ruadhán's monastery, and the sound of the bell of each used to be heard in both places, until blessed Bréanainn, prompted by divine inspiration, one day said to his brethren: 'I shall leave this district to Ruadhán, and go to another province'. Bréanainn sought Ruadhán's blessing and prayer, and the saint blessed him and his journey. Bréanainn then proceeded to the province of Connacht and founded there his own monastic town of Clonfert, in which he himself is buried.

5 ~ Another time, blessed father Ruadhán, wishing to spread the word of God among the people, commended his monastery of Lorrha to holy men, and went off with some monks to the northern part of Ireland, where he performed many miracles in the name of God and founded a large *parochia*.

6 ~ Ruadhán wished to build a church in a particular place, but a certain man, who owned the property, prevented that church being built, and insulted the holy man of God greatly. On being addressed by Ruadhán, he grasped the hand of the man of God and, dragging him away, expelled him with insult from the place. The saint of God put up with this patiently, but Christ quickly took vengeance for the insult, for at that same hour sand and sea covered over the property, and from that day until now the place is uninhabitable.

7 ~ Another time, when Ruadhán had come to a monastic town called Slanore in the territory of Cairbre Mhór, that same hour the dead chieftain of the region was brought to his settlement, with his entire people about him, mourning. On seeing Ruadhán, these made doleful complaint with a loud cry concerning the death of their chieftain, and the saint, moved by their misery, took pity on them. Approaching the bier, he prayed full of faith to Christ for the soul of the chieftain and, at his prayer, the chieftain immediately arose unharmed and, thanking God and Ruadhán, he greeted all. Knowing that he had been revived through Ruadhán's prayer, he granted both the aforementioned monastic town of Slanore and his own territory in perpetuity to God and to Ruadhán.

8 ~   On a certain day, when Ruadhán came to a place called Ros Éinne in the
territory of Oirthir, he found a large group of its people gathered there, and
he questioned them as to what they were doing. They replied, saying: 'In this
fort there was a treasure in which was much of our wealth, and it has been
buried and hidden in this field for a long time, but we do not know where,
and we can hardly upturn the whole field. We ask of you, therefore, servant
of God, through Christ, that you show us where it is in the name of the Lord'.
Having been entreated in the name of God, Ruadhán then went and made
a circle about the place. Marking the ground with his staff, he blessed it and
prayed and, when he came to where the treasure was, the ground immediately
opened up and great wealth came into view. The people then gave thanks to
God and granted the aforesaid fort, with its inhabitants, to Ruadhán. The
holy man of God established a church and left there holy men of his disciples.

9 ~   After this and other miracles, Ruadhán left the north and came to the south
of Ireland, where he built churches for God in the same way, and many miracles
were performed through him. As he made his way, he came to a sister of his
called Dairí who lived in the lands of Uí Oilealla. The inhabitants of that
territory granted a certain place to Ruadhán and the holy man built a
monastery there named Shancough.

10 ~ Some time or other, a certain kitchen servant of Ruadhán's monastery was
carrying milk on a horse from the cattle-shed to the monastery. But over
seven days the milk was spilled daily on to the ground as he entered the
gateway of the monastic town. On another day, holy father Ruadhán, wishing
to know where this evil was from, went out so that he might get to know its
cause. He saw in the gateway two demons, one on the right, the other on the
left, with iron hammers in their hands with which they struck the vessels so
that they fell broken on to the ground. When Ruadhán asked the demons as
to why they dared to inflict this evil on the servants of Christ, they confessed,
saying: 'We dare to inflict this evil on you on account of the wickedness of
the servant who has willed it'. When this was said, Ruadhán sent the demons
to the bottom of a nearby lake, and ordered them in the name of God to
remain there, harming nobody; and thus it was done, as the holy man of God
ordained.

11 ~ A certain young man of the people called Araidh Chliach in the region of
Munster, who wished to study medicine, came to Ruadhán to ask him to

bless his hands, eyes and mind. Ruadhán blessed his eyes and mind and therewith he became expert in the art of medicine.

12 ~ At that time, the wife of a nobleman of the region of Cuala, near the sea in the eastern part of Leinster, was plagued by an incurable disease, and the fifty medical doctors attending on her could not bring back any of her health. Afterwards, the lady abandoned all medical men and commended herself to Christ, and to Ruadhán who lived far away from her. An angel of the Lord then came to Ruadhán, to say: 'The wife of a nobleman in the region of Cuala has a bad illness and there is no way in which the doctors could cure her, but God allowed her, whose illness is unknown to doctors, to receive health through you; she has in her womb a bleeding birth, and cannot bring forth'. Thereupon, through the will of God, Ruadhán showed himself with a clear light on a certain night to that lady in a vision during her sleep, and said to her: 'Do not fear, for I shall make you healthy in the name of Christ, and I shall send to you a certain youth who will cure you, and you will not be cured by the other doctors, as you began to deny those who cannot bring any medicine to bear on you'. After this, he receded from her and, on the following day, Ruadhán called a certain youth to him, blessed water and spat some of his own saliva into it, before saying to the youth: 'Go to the kingdom of Leinster and assist the noble lady of the region of Cuala, who is ill and hopes for the pity of Christ through me'. The brother obediently accepted the water in a bronze vessel from the hand of the man of God, and set out on a long journey to the noble lady, to give her the water blessed by Ruadhán. Rejoicing, the noble lady then drank the water and poured it over her body and, with that, what was in her womb became liquified and disappeared. Released from her travails and made healthy and unharmed, she then gave thanks to God and to Ruadhán. While the noble lady wished to send rewards to Ruadhán, his servant refused them all, except a certain linen cloth of hers, which lay on the altar of Ruadhán's monastery at Lorrha for a long time. Ruadhán had ordered it thus as the youth was going on his way.

13 ~ At another time, Bréanainn's boat sank in the Shannon Estuary in the western part of Ireland, near the ocean, and the son of the king of Britain, asleep in the prow of the boat, went down with it. Bréanainn then said to some disciples: 'Go quickly to Ruadhán and ask him to come on my behalf, for God granted to him that he raise up our boat and resuscitate the drowned youth'. On hearing them, Ruadhán immediately went off with them to Bréanainn and,

on his praying where the boat sank, it rose forthwith from the depths of the
estuary and came to land where the saint was. It was the same with the king's
son who had drowned; he rose from the depths of the sea, saying that holy
Ruadhán's staff was about him and that he was revived by him. The virtues,
then, of the two saints are shown by this miracle; namely Bréanainn's prophecy
and the power of Ruadhán's prayer. And he who was drowned lived for many
a day afterwards.

14 ~ There were fifty monks with Ruadhán in the monastery of Lorrha to whom
almighty God provided food without any work save prayer and genuflections;
for there was then a certain tree in the courtyard of the monastery whose sap
sufficed for the aforesaid monks and guests. The juice of this tree was very
sweet and satisfied all who partook of it as food and drink, and monks fled
from their churches all over Ireland to the place in which, as they heard, there
was so much of God's grace. Thereupon, with the above-mentioned monks
and guests partaking of nothing but the sap of the tree and herbs, the indignant
saints of Ireland, having formed a plan, requested of Ruadhán's master Finnian
that he ask his pupil to cease, together with his monks, from this leisurely
life, lest it be a cause of muttering for those whose monks were fleeing to
Ruadhán. At the command of the saints of Ireland, holy father Finnian then
set out from his monastery of Clonard to Lorrha, where, with Ruadhán's
permission, he blessed the tree with the sign of the holy cross, upon which
the tree stopped exuding its sap. On this being done, the cellarer said to
Ruadhán: 'What will the monks and guests eat and drink tonight?' The saint
replied: 'Almighty God will send us food; pour water, therefore, into your
vessels and, on account of my father Finnian, the power of Christ will convert
it to wine'. Everything turned out in this way; indeed, as the cellarer himself
was drawing water with his servants from the little river of the monastery, a
fish of amazing size, enough to sate the inhabitants of the place on that night,
broke through a stone on which its trace remains to this day. The water was
then converted to the power and taste of wine and, while glorifying his saints,
all gave thanks to God. Afterwards, Finnian blessed the fields of the monastery
of Lorrha, while saying to its monks: 'Pray to God and work the land and,
without any laying of dung for fertilizing, it will give its harvest forever as a
gift from God'; and thus it remains. Then, with the saints blessing each other,
Finnian went back on his way in peace, while Ruadhán, commanding his
monks to live as others, remained in his monastery of Lorrha.

11 Early remains at Pollrone, Co. Kilkenny. These formed part of the possessions of the house of Augustinian canonesses at Kilculliheen, which was founded by Diarmuid Mac Murchadha in 1151 (image courtesy of Dani Horton).

15 ~ At that time, there was a powerful and peacemaking king in Ireland by the name of Diarmuid son of Cearbhall, who reigned in Tara. This man made a most binding peace in his kingdom, and ordained that no one should dare to give another even a box on the ear in anger. But the king's steward set out for the province of Connacht, to the kingdom of Uí Mhaine, and with him was his herald, who had been persuaded by the devil not to go into forts until they were broken up, so as to allow him to enter with a spear transverse in his mouth, thus broadcasting the king's authority over another realm. On coming then to a certain fort, it was destroyed for him, as we said above, for fear of steward and king, who, however, did not know of it. But, when the lord of the aforesaid fort came home and saw the entrance to his fort destroyed, he was so filled with an intolerable rage that he killed the herald and, for fear of the king, he then left his homeland with all of his people and came to the kingdom of Múscraighe in the province of Munster, to a certain holy bishop named Seanach. That lord and daring warrior, who killed the aforesaid herald, was called Aodh, and his mother and Seanach's mother were two sisters, but the blessed bishop, not wishing to have the guilty one with him, led him to

Ruadhán so that he might protect him. Ruadhán, wishing to help him in his misery, accepted him under his protection, for the saint's two sisters, Caol and Ruadhnaid, had reared Bishop Seanach. King Diarmuid, on hearing of the killing of a man in his kingdom, became furious, however, and sent pursuers after the slayer so that he might not remain alive. On discovering that Aodh had taken flight to Britain, king Diarmuid then sent his legation to the king of Britain so as to ensure that Aodh could not stay there. At this, not daring to be in Britain, Aodh returned secretly to Ruadhán in Ireland, and was hidden by the saint in a certain pit in the ground, which was, however, told to the king by jealous evildoers. On learning of this, the king came to Ruadhán in order to carry Aodh away from him. Now, as we said above, Ruadhán built many churches and the one he was in when the king set out for him was at Pollrone on the bank of the River Suir in the southern part of Ossory, near the kingdom of the Déise. On arriving at Ruadhán's aforesaid place, the king sent in his warriors so that they might bring Aodh out to him, but when his charioteer entered the church ahead of all, his eyes were blinded, after which the others returned to the king in fear. The king himself, knowing that Ruadhán would not tell a lie, then went in and questioned him, saying: 'Where is Aodh, the king's guilty one?' The saint replied: 'I know not, unless he's underneath you'; for the king was then standing over the pit in which Aodh was. The king, without questioning Ruadhán further, then went away a good distance from the church, before he brought to mind and scrutinized the saint's words, namely: 'I know not, unless he's underneath you'. At that, the king returned to the aforesaid place and, having lit a torch, ordered one of his warriors, Donnán by name, to dig out the pit in which Aodh was, but when Donnán raised an arm with the hoe, his arm withered immediately, and he remained immobile. On doing penance, this same soldier Donnán was cured, and with him the charioteer who was blinded, and these received the holy habit from father Ruadhán, and lived afterwards in great sanctity. These two well-known saints, whose lives offered good example to many, are buried in the said monastery of Pollrone.

16 ~ King Diarmuid then entered the monastery, took Aodh from the pit and commanded his men to take him to his town of Tara so that all might witness his torments. However, Ruadhán struck his bell over the king and, still wishing to protect Aodh, he went with the king to Tara, accompanied by Bréanainn. On arriving in Tara, saints Ruadhán and Bréanainn, having raised up their bells, sang while fasting against the king but, on the first night, the king,

making little of it, did not hear them. During that night, however, the twelve sons of twelve chieftains of Ireland, who were being fostered by the king in Tara, and greatly loved by him, died. Great mourning then broke out in the hall of the king and, at his coming, the foster-parents and parents said: 'Ruadhán killed our sons'. Then, on the following day, the foster-parents came in mourning to Ruadhán, and made a piteous complaint before him concerning the deaths of innocent boys. In truth, the saint, moved by pity, prayed to the Lord for them and, while he was praying, the twelve little boys rose from the dead. Those who saw that great miracle were filled with fear, and they glorified Christ's grace in Ruadhán, but the king had no wish to relax the law of his realm.

17 ~ The saints then fasted and prayed against the king and he, on learning of this, fasted and prayed against the saints so that, with the king himself fasting and praying, the saints could do nothing to him. This king was a peacemaking protector of his country, a helper of churches and monks, truthful in speech, even-handed in judgment, and firm in faith. On a certain night, the saints pretended to eat and yet did not do so; accordingly, thinking the saints were eating, the king himself ate and slept that night, and had a dream in which he saw a wonderful tree that stretched as far as heaven, in the shadow of which stood Ireland. He saw twelve elders with their disciples to the number of 150 cutting the tree down with axes, and one of them, more forceful than all others, cut at it until it fell to the ground, making a sound that woke the terrified king from his dream, with the noise of the synod in song filling his ears. At that, now divinely inspired, the king knew the sense of all his vision; namely, that he himself, who governed Ireland, had sown that tree; and that those twelve elders cutting at it with others were Ruadhán and Bréanainn with ten other holy fathers and their disciples, Ruadhán being the more forceful of them in cutting the tree; and that the fall of the tree, marking the end of his life and reign, was given by God to the saints. Thus did the king interpret the dream to his friends and, on coming himself to the saints who were holding vigil, he said to them: 'I have made kingdoms strong, and a firm law in every place that there might be lasting peace for churches and people everywhere, and I defend the good according to the law of Christ, but you exercise evil, by protecting one guilty of death. From a little, moreover, many things arise'. Turning to Ruadhán, the king then said to him: 'For this thing that you did, Ruadhán, you will receive punishment from the Holy Trinity, for your *parochia* will be the first in Ireland to fail'. Diarmuid and Ruadhán

then mutually engaged in a miserable conflict, with the saint saying to the king: 'Your kingdom will first fail and none of your seed will ever reign'. The king replied: 'Your much-loved place will be deserted, and swine will turn it over with their snouts'. Ruadhán continued: 'This royal town of yours at Tara, in which the kingdom of Ireland has been ruled for many years, will be empty hundreds of years before'. The king responded: 'Your body will bear a stain from this day and one of your limbs will perish, and one of your eyes will never see the light'. Ruadhán said: 'Your body will be slain by enemies, and your limbs will be separated from one another'. Finally, the king said: 'A fierce wild boar will dig out your coffin with his tooth', and Ruadhán replied: 'Your thigh-bone, which was not raised before me, will not be buried with your body, but a day will come when a certain man will throw it on top of his basin in the dung-heap of his sheep'. When the king then noticed that Ruadhán had said worse things of him, he turned to all the saints and said: 'Ye, fathers, truly defend iniquity; I, however, defend the truth in God's name. You have destroyed me, and you have brought loss to my kingdom; God loves you, however, for your merits more than me, but I shall trust in the mercy of my God; go, then, and take this free man with you, and return a fee to the kingdom for him'. The holy men joyfully heard these words.

18 ~ Afterwards, thirty hyacinth-coloured horses appearing out of the sea came to Tara, and boldly passed by all as far as Ruadhán, who then said to the king: 'Take these distinguished and swift horses sent by God in payment for your captive'. The king then gave the horses to the chieftains and rulers of Ireland, after which he and the saint, now at peace, prayed for one another, but what they had said earlier to one another in conflict was truly put into force daily. With Aodh set free, Ruadhán returned placated from Tara to his own people, and the aforementioned horses returned after a short while to the sea from which they came.

19 ~ When Ruadhán had retired out of Tara, some lepers met him on the way, requesting that he give them alms, and he gave them the horses of his wagon. Two deer immediately came from a nearby wood and placed their tamed necks meekly under the saint's wagon; they then set out in this way with Ruadhán until he arrived at his church.

20 ~ On a certain day, as Ruadhán and his disciples were making a journey, they discovered a tree lying across the road so that they could not draw the wagon

along. On seeing this, Ruadhán blessed the tree with the sign of the holy cross, and it immediately rose up, and subsequently stood erect for a long time.

21 ~ On another occasion, Ruadhán ordered his monks to eat meat on the arrival of holy guests, but there was a certain former layman who, while at supper with the brethren, did not wish to eat meat for hospitality's sake. The bread he was eating appeared to all, however, as if it were raw and bloody meat; on noticing this, Ruadhán blessed a part of the meat they were eating and turned it into bread in front of the ex-layman who then did penance in front of the holy men and was saved. Then, when Ruadhán blessed the raw and bloody meat that, because of the ex-layman's inobedience, replaced the bread in his hand, it changed back to bread. On seeing such things, the holy guests and brethren were strengthened in their love of God and of Ruadhán.

22 ~ On a certain day in summer, when the ground had dried up, twelve lepers came to Ruadhán to ask alms of him. The saint then pressed his staff upon the ground, and a clear well immediately rose up out of it, from which he made a pond before ordering the lepers to wash themselves in it. On washing themselves, all the lepers came out of the water cleansed of their leprosy and, on seeing themselves cleansed, they gave thanks to God and to Ruadhán. That pond is called by Ruadhán's name up to this day.

23 ~ Once, with the unexpected arrival of guests on a cold day, Ruadhán ordered his disciples to light a fire quickly for those who were frozen. When, however, no receptacle had been immediately found in which to bring fire to the guesthouse, holy father Ruadhán, glowing with affection, placed fire with his own hands in the lap of a disciple, and not only were the latter's clothes not burnt, the colour of his clothes was also unaffected.

24 ~ A certain hind used to come about sunset to Ruadhán over a long period and be milked for him; the same hind, having run quickly over the long journey, used to come early on the following day to Colmán Eala, to be milked for him. In this way, the hind dwelt between the two holy men who lived from its milk.

25 ~ Another time, when Ruadhán had been residing with his monks in a church formerly called Doire Eidhneach – but now known as Derrynaflan, a place

in which religious men always dwell – on the boundary of the kingdoms of
Éile and Eoghanacht, holy Bishop Colmán son of Daráine, then living in a
place called Longfordpass, sent a receptacle full of butter to Ruadhán and
his monks in a wagon drawn by two oxen. There is a large and extremely wet
bog between the two aforesaid places, known as the bog of the lake of Lurga,
where there was formerly a lake in which there was a most venomous beast
that killed many. A certain strong hero named Fear Domhain split it in two
with one blow of his sword, but the hind part of the beast, swimming to him
through the water, cut him through the stomach to the ground so that he
died; he was of the race of the Leinstermen, and it is said that he killed six
hundred warriors in one battle. But, when the oxen arrived at the bog, they
discovered in it a smooth and very hard roadway, which no one ever found
there before or after, as far as Ruadhán's church. From the beginning of spring
until Pentecost, the receptacle of butter was divided by Ruadhán among 150
monks with their guests and, through God's gift, it was found to be full on
the day of Pentecost.

26 ~ Once, when the holy elder Ruadhán was in a certain place, a woman came to
him in tears to ask that he raise from the dead her deceased son in Christ's
name. On seeing her misery, the holy elder prayed to God for him and, as he
prayed, the boy rose from the dead and the saint gave him alive to his mother.

27 ~ The most holy elder Ruadhán resuscitated another boy through the grace of
God in the region of Uí Luighdheach. When the boy was placed under holy
Ruadhán's cloak, he immediately rose from the dead and lived on for a long
time.

28 ~ The most blessed elder Ruadhán also revived a third boy from the dead in
the kingdom of Éile, at a place formerly called Cuilleann but now known as
Tullaroan. The father of the resuscitated son then gave both him and the
place to God and to Ruadhán.

29 ~ There was a most evil man in the kingdom of Midhe by the name of
Éighmheach, who once gave Bishop Aodh son of Breac a site on which to
build a church for God. The bishop then promised the kingdom of heaven
to that impious man, but the man afterwards died and demons took him
away with them. Bishop Aodh, wishing to fulfil in God what he had promised,
then asked of Christ that he be allowed to fight for his soul in the air against

the demons. When the demons had overcome the holy bishop and had begun to drag away the soul of the miserable man from him, Aodh called Ruadhán and Colum Cille to his assistance and these, on hearing him spiritually from afar, came swiftly to him at the same time as the man died. There they overcame the demons and brought the soul of the aforesaid man to rest, but only almighty God and the saints know the mystery of the affair. On coming down from the sky, the holy men then greeted one another before each of them ran at the sound of his own bell ringing. In this way, Colum Cille, who had in his hand a writing-board of a colour that glittered as gold, for what he used to write, gave it to Ruadhán. One day, however, at a time when Colum Cille was staying on the island of Iona, Baoithín, Colum's successor, questioned him, saying: 'Where is your writing-board, which you had for a long time?' Colum replied: 'When I, Ruadhán, and Bishop Aodh were repulsing demons on behalf of the soul of a miserable man, I placed it in Ruadhán's hand'. As Baoithín was marvelling at this, Colum said to him: 'Let you now go to Ruadhán in Ireland, and you will find my writing-board with him, and bring it back here with you'. Ruadhán, foreseeing prophetically the arrival of Baoithín while he was still on his way, ordered that the necessary things be prepared for him. Baoithín found everything as Colum had prophesied and, with a kiss of peace, returned from Ruadhán.

30 ~ After this and other similar miracles, our most holy elder Ruadhán began in most venerable old age to sicken to death, whereupon many holy men gathered for his passing. Now, since he was born of a race of kings, father Ruadhán had a regal form, the length of his body being twelve feet; externally handsome and more beautiful internally; he was noble according to men, but more noble according to God; great in body, but even greater in grace; large in front of men, but even larger in front of God; full of love and humility, patience, mercy and other good works. For all of these good things, our patron Ruadhán received great glory from God and men. The most blessed elder Ruadhán departed for heaven on 15 April, and his body was buried with honour by the holy fathers in his monastic town of Lorrha. God's miracles are performed through his remains for all time; he has honour and everlasting reward in heaven in the presence of the Eternal Father and Jesus Christ his son, our Lord, and the Holy Spirit, the Paraclete, to which three-in-one God there is honour and glory forever and ever. Amen.

Thus ends the Life of holy Ruadhán, bishop and confessor.

Notes to the Lives

LIFE OF COLUM OF TERRYGLASS

§1 *His father Nainnidh was a powerful king and his mother was called Mionchlú.* Of Nainnidh son of Nastar, the powerful king, nothing else is recorded, but his son Cormac was regarded as the progenitor of two Uí Chriomhthannáin families, the Uí Mhaoil Ochtraigh and the Uí Dhuibh (Ó Muraíle, *The great book*, 483.1–5). The name of the saint's mother was also rendered Mionchloth (Ó Riain, *Corpus*, §722.20). R describes Nainnidh as a powerful man only.

§2 *was seen to glow in flames.* There is another example of this common motif in Mochaomhóg's Life (§7). See also Ó hAodha, *Bethu Brigte*, 1 §1; Stokes, *Lives of the saints*, 1911–26 (p. 205).

§3 *heat and brightness.* R reads *odore*, 'aroma', for *ardore*, 'heat' in S.

§3 *Momhaodhóg.* This saint's pedigree also attaches him to the Uí Chriomhthannáin (Ó Riain, *Corpus*, §242.1; *DIS* 494–5). As is shown by the litanies of Irish saints, the topos of seven bishops was a common one (Plummer, *Irish litanies*, 68–74).

§4 *Colmán Cúile.* Like Momhaodhóg and Colum, Colmán Cúile is attached by the genealogists to the Uí Chriomhthannáin; his church of Clonkeen was located in the Laois parish of Clonenagh, within the *samhadh*, 'congregation', of Fiontan of Clonenagh. For Colmán, see *DIS* 203, and also the note below on the Life of Crónán of Roscrea (§20).

§4 *that holy school.* As Charles Plummer pointed out, the school at Clonard was perhaps the most famous of all, especially as far as mention in the Lives of the saints is concerned (*VSHP* i, cxv). The canons regular, whose priory at Clonard was founded in 1144, would have been especially eager to promote this view of their church (Gwynn and Hadcock, *Medieval religious houses*, 163).

§5 *one ... of twelve.* Mention of the number twelve evokes the idea of the twelve Irish apostles, who included Colum of Terryglass, Colum Cille and others. For lists of those who studied with the two Colums at Clonard, see *VSHH* 83 §5, 102 §19.

§5 *sons of kings.* Colum's father is described as a 'powerful king' in §1 above. For Colum Cille's claim to royal descent, see *VSHH* 366 §1. Adhamhnán simply states that he was born of noble parents (Anderson, *Adomnán's Life*, 186).

§6 *his fingers shone.* There are several other examples of this motif in Irish Lives, as, for example, in Muirchú's Life of Patrick, in the Life of Seanán of Scattery and, remarkably, since it relates to a man who died as recently as 1081–2, in the Life written in Regensburg for Marianus Scottus (Bieler, *The Patrician texts*, 116; *VSHH* 310 §11; Weber, *Iren auf dem Kontinent*, 333–46). As against Seanán, who raised his left hand, Colum raises his right one. See also *VSHP* i, cxxxviii (n. 7).

§7 *relics of Peter and Paul.* The relics of these two apostles are said also to have been brought to Ireland by Molaise of Devenish and Tighearnach of Clones (*VSHP* ii, 137 §24; 263 §5). Both places contained priories of canons regular, a group that was particularly devoted to Peter and Paul (Gwynn and Hadcock, *Medieval religious houses*, 164, 169; Ó Riain, *Feastdays*, 223).

§7 *the city of Martin.* The city intended here is Tours in France. Among other saints said to have visited Tours on the way to or from Rome are Molaise of Devenish (*VSHP* ii, 136 §21), Tighearnach of Clones (*VSHP* ii, 263 §5), Seanán of Scattery (Stokes, *Lives of the saints*, 2044–58) and Ciarán of Tubbrid (Power, *Life of St Declan*, 58), Colum Cille (Herbert, *Iona, Kells and Derry*, 231).

§7 *Colum elevated the relics.* Elevation (Latin *elevatio*) was a technical term used of the raising of relics following their discovery (Latin *inventio*). Elevation was usually followed by enshrinement of the relics and by their translation (Latin *translatio*), either within the same church or to another church elsewhere.

§7 *chrismal and robe.* The chrismal held the holy oil used in baptism or anointing, whereas the robe (Latin *trabea*) probably refers to a vestment worn by the saint, perhaps even to the famous cloak shared by him with a beggar. Such non-bodily relics, known as *brandea*, were highly prized. Among other saints said to have brought relics of Martin to Ireland were Ciarán of Seirkieran and Maodhóg of Ferns and Drumlane (*BNÉ* i, 122 §62; 266 §232). Both Colum Cille (Herbert, *Iona, Kells and Derry*, 231 §35) and Seanán (Stokes, *Lives of the saints*, 2044–58) are reputed to have brought Martin's gospel-book to Ireland, one to Derry, the other to Scattery. The Derry copy, which was also allegedly taken from Martin's grave, is mentioned in the annals (*AU* 1166, 1182; cf. Herbert, *Iona, Kells and Derry*, 190–1; Cunningham and Gillespie, 'The Uí Dhomhnaill and their books', 486).

§8 *They fasted for three days and nights.* A fast over three days was a stock element, often used in Ireland in relation to the 'cleansing of sites' during consecration of churches. Plummer (*VSHP* i, cxx) cites other examples from Bede (Colgrave and Mynors, *Bede's Ecclesiastical history*, 297–9), and from the Lives of Ailbhe (§29), Fionnbharr (§12) and Déaglán (§22). Cf. Ó Riain, 'Another Cork charter', 4.

§8   *a shrine decorated in gold and silver.* According to the Life of St Eligius of Noyon, he was commissioned by the Merovingian king Dagobert I (d. 639) to make a shrine for Martin's remains, decorated in gold and gems (Jacobsen, 'Saints' tombs', 1109n.).

§9   *three men died.* This may echo the belief, as recounted by Gregory of Tours, that Martin raised three men from the dead (Dalton, *The history of the Franks*, ii, 24 (I.39)).

§10   *the part of Britain in which were Saxons.* The part intended is probably the area about London. This area is also singled out in the the Life of Abán (*VSHP* i, 11–12 §§13–14), probably with a view to rebutting the claims of the Anglo-Normans concerning the need for reform in the Irish church by showing how it was the Irish who converted the English. Cf. Ó Riain, 'St Abbán', 165.

§12   *His brother Cairbre.* This is Cairbre son of Nainnidh from whom, according to the Book of Leinster genealogies, descended the Uí Mhaoile Tola (O'Brien, *Corpus*, 315ab35). In that text, Cairbre's name occurs immediately after the pedigree of Aodh Mac Criomhthainn, coarb of Colum and chief scribe of the Book of Leinster.

§12   *Eadarghabhal.* This may be Addergoole in the parish of Aghmacart, later the site of a nunnery belonging to the Augustinian canonesses at Kilculliheen: see above at p. 6.

§12   *a pilgrim named Crónán.* This man may be commemorated at Kilcronan in the parish of Dysartgallen, Co. Laois. See above at p. 6.

§§13–14 *three disciples.* These sections, with much the same wording, are also in the Life of Fiontan of Clonenagh, from which they may have been borrowed (*VSHP* ii, 97–8 §§4–5; *VSHH* 146 §3; *DIS* 339–41; Sperber, 'One saint, two fathers', 176). Of the three saints, Caomhán of Anatrim (*DIS* 155) also figures in the Life of Mochaomhóg (§§10–11). For Mochaoimhe, alias Nadh Caoimhe, see *DIS* 459.

§13   *Mobhí of the Maca Alla.* The place intended here is Cloney in Co. Kildare, whose saint, Baodán (alias Mobhaoi) of the Maca Alla (*DIS* 85–6), was reputedly also a cousin of Crónán of Roscrea, as the latter's Life (§2) explains. R omits *Maca Alla*.

§14   *Séadna by name.* This boy is otherwise unidentified.

§14   *Fiontan came to the place.* The purpose of the biographer here would appear to be to bring together the churches of Clonenagh and Terryglass, to both of which the Mac Criomhthainn family provided abbots. See also Sperber, 'One saint, two fathers', 176–9.

§15 *Tír Snámha*. Tír Snámha has yet to be identified but it must lie in Uí Mhaine, which corresponded approximately to the diocese of Clonfert in east Galway. It seems near Lough Derg, and perhaps at or near Snámh Dá Éan, a crossing place of the River Shannon between Clonmacnoise and Clonburren.

§15 *740*. This number, omitted in R, is written in Roman numerals as *.d.cc.xl.*

§15 *Aurraith Tophiloc and Toim Boinden*. Neither place has been identified, but the archaic character of the spelling would suggest that both names were taken from an earlier written document, possibly a charter relating to the possessions of Terryglass. R omits the names.

§15 *Mac Reithe*. The spelling *Mac Criche* in the text probably reflects the erroneous belief that *creach*, 'plunder, booty', was the second element of the name, as is specifically stated in the saint's own Life (Plummer, *Miscellanea*, 15 §10, 55; cf. *DIS* 420–3).

§16 *a certain tree*. According to his Life (§14), Ruadhán also had a lime-tree that sated the whole community, in his case continuously until it became an object of envy on the part of other saints.

§17 *Why should birds avoid a bird*. Lying behind this assertion is the common (but mistaken) notion that the name Colum was derived from Latin *columba*, 'dove'. In fact, it is a native name that generated numerous hypocoristic or pet forms (Ó Riain, 'Cainnech *alias* Colum Cille', 20–35).

§19 *disciples, Nadh Caoimhe and Fiontan*. According to §14 above, Fiontan had already left Colum to go to Clonenagh. In the same paragraph, however, Colum foretold that he and Nadh Caoimhe would be together in Terryglass.

§19 *Terryglass*. Despite his regular association with this church, Colum gets no closer to Terryglass in the text than his sight of it from the lake.

§20 *Shannon Estuary*. Latin *Mare ... quod dicitur Luimnech*, 'The sea which is called Limerick'. This name, sometimes with *fretum*, 'channel, estuary', replacing *mare*, 'sea', is also used for the Shannon Estuary in other texts, such as the Life of Ruadhán (§14). Cf. *VSHP* ii, 334 'Lu(i)mnech'.

§20 *Island of Earc*. Latin *Insula Erci*. As Kenneth Nicholls points out to me, the abbey of Canon Island and two quarters of land called 'Chanons Island, Inisherke, Inishloe and Inisht[ibered]' are listed among the possessions of Donough O'Brien, fourth earl of Thomond in 1619 (PHA MS B.26.T.16/V.16). Elsewhere (*Fiants* under 1775), 'Innysherke' and the two other islands are placed 'nigh to the Isle of Channons'. This proximity is borne out by Thomas Dingly's drawing of nearby Crovraghan Castle in the Fergus Estuary, which shows 'Enish Sherkey' separated from 'Cannons Island' by one other island only, called 'Enish

Mac ony' (Breen-Ua Cróinín, 'Some tower houses', 8). This would suggest that *Insula Erci*, later 'Inisherke', formed part of the possessions of the canons regular on Canon Island. The Irish Life of Finnian of Clonard refers to the place variously as *Inis Mac nIndeirc* and *Inis Mac nEirc* (Stokes, *Lives of the saints*, l. 2770, p. 230).

§20   *Three orders of men … Agha*. The text uses *longitudo*, 'length', to measure the distance between the various places. Agha, here mentioned for the first (and last) time, lay within the territory of the Uí Dhróna, later Idrone in Co. Carlow. It was among the possessions of the diocese of Leighlin, and was located not far from Lorum, a church elsewhere associated with Colum of Terryglass (Sheehy, *Pontificia*, i, 129–30; Ó Riain, *Corpus*, §§667–8). It may be that the Mac Criomhthainn family also had an association with Agha.

§21   '*Colum's stone*'. I know of no other mention of this place, nor am I aware of any other tradition to the effect that Colum's relics were brought to the Land of Promise.

§22   *Tradraighe*. Tradraighe, anglicized Tradree, comprised several parishes, including Tomfinlough of which Luchtighearn was patron (McCotter, *Medieval Ireland*, 191–2).

§22   *Luchtighearn*. Luchtighearn of Tomfinlough (*DIS* 406–7) also figures in the Life of Mochaomhóg (§10), which depicts him as a disciple of Comhghall of Bangor.

§24   R omits this paragraph.

§24   *Neasán*. For Neasán's meeting with Patrick, which makes no mention of a shepherd from the East, see Mulchrone, *Bethu Phátraic*, 2400–6 (= Stokes, *The tripartite Life*, 204). As explained above (p. 7), his encounter with Colum may reflect a possible connection between his church of Mungret (south-east of the Island of Earc) and the canons regular of St Augustine.

§24   *Ailbhe said the same*. For Neasán's visit to Ailbhe, which again makes no mention of Colum, see *VSHH* 129–30 §50; cf. *DIS* 514–15.

§25   *another island*. There are many islands in this part of the estuary, including Canon Island and others mentioned at §20 above.

§26   The Latin and Irish recensions of the Life of Finnian make little of this episode and its sequel. In the Latin version (*VSHH* 102 §20), Finnian is credited with a prophecy to the effect that Colum would render him the last rites. In the Irish version (Stokes, *Lives of the saints*, 2769–73, p. 230), Finnian receives the last rites from Colum, who is brought from the island in the Shannon Estuary. Neither version refers to Colum's subsequent death in Clonee.

§27   *Clonee ... a pupil of his.* A saint named Colmán, doubtless a double of Colum himself, is associated with Clonee (Ó Riain, *Corpus*, §707.210). R appears to name the pupil, corruptly, as *episcopus Cullen*.

§27   *Luchtighearn.* This saint's presence fulfils the prophecy made by Colum at §22 above.

§27   *I did not procure.* As pointed out by Heist, the text that would explain why Luchtighearn did not wish to join Colum is evidently missing. R reads at this point: *si tibi placet nolo nunc de corpore exire quia adhuc tecum ire non monui sed adhuc maiora opera augere cupio*, 'if it pleases you, I do not wish to leave my body now because I did not bring to mind hitherto to go with you, but I desire to increase previous good works'.

§28   *Nadh Caoimhe ... Odhrán.* For Nadh Caoimhe, see above at §§13, 19. R writes the name as *maccumius/maccomius*. Odhrán (*DIS* 519) was associated with Latteragh in the Tipperary barony of Upper Ormond, a church later affiliated to the Augustinian priory of Toomyvara (Gwynn and Gleeson, *A history*, 473). The prophecy is also attested in Ciarán's Life (*VSHP* i, 227–8 §25; *BNÉ* i, 121 §§54–5), as well as in verse attributed to Bréanainn of Clonfert (*MartT* 118–19; *MartO*' clxxxii). Sperber emphasizes a divergence between the verse – which prefers M(o)chaoimhe to Nadh Caoimhe and refers to the 'border of Eachtgha (Slieve Aughty)' – and the Life, which uses the form Nadh Caoimhe and mentions a stop-over in Clonmacnoise only. It should be noted, however, that in both cases the divergence can be explained *metri causa* (Sperber, 'One saint, two fathers', 184–6).

§28   *lands of the Uí Néill.* R reads: *per fines Midensium*.

§28   *Clonmacnoise.* A priory of Augustinian canons was established at Clonmacnoise, already, perhaps, by the middle of the twelfth century (Gwynn and Hadcock, *Medieval religious houses*, 153, 165).

§29   *Aonghas.* Bearing a name also written as Aona, Aonghas is said to have been Ciarán's immediate successor at Clonmacnoise (*DIS* 77).

§29   *select this place.* The corrector of the text added *non* before *eligit* as, without it, the text would make little sense. Early in the Life (§19 above), Colum had specifically referred to Terryglass as the place of his resurrection.

§29   *Ciarán will precede.* In the litany of the Stowe Missal, which was kept at Lorrha, near Terryglass, the names of the two Ciaráns, of Clonmacnoise and Seirkieran, precede the names of the two Colums, presumably of Iona and Terryglass, with the names of the two Brendans in-between (Warner, *The Stowe Missal*, ii, 14).

§30 *Colmán Beag.* Colmán Beag, son of Diarmuid, a brother of Colmán Mór, eponymous ancestor of the powerful Clann Cholmáin of Midhe (now mainly Westmeath), is probably intended (*AU* 587, 593). R uses *paruus*, 'small', in place of *modicus* in S. For a discussion of the two brothers, see O'Flynn, 'The two Colmáns'.

§31 *Colum's remains were placed ... in a preordained spot.* As far as I am aware, there is no record of the site reputed to have been Colum's grave.

LIFE OF CRÓNÁN OF ROSCREA

§1 *cairn of An Mhagh.* Text: *ab aceruo an Mhaighe*; this name, if it is such, has not been identified. As Plummer points out, the name in its fully Irish form might be 'Carn *or* Ulaidh an Maighe' (*VSHP* ii, 335). The name Ánmhagh, genitive Ánmhaighe, is also attested, but not in Éile (Ó Riain, Ó Murchadha and Murray, *Historical dictionary*, i, 58).

§1 *the Crónán whose Life.* S describes Crónán as the 'principal' son of the three.

§1 *When persecution ... sons of Odhrán.* This is omitted by S.

§1 *church of the sons of Odhrán.* Text: *cella filiorum Odhrani*; this place has not been identified.

§2 *their possessions.* In S, these are described as the 'contemptible vanities of the world'.

§2 *and of his mother's sister.* S uses the term *consobrinus*, 'cousin (on the mother's side)', to describe the relationship. Mobhaoi, alias Baodán, was principally remembered as patron of Cloney in the parish of Kilberry, Co. Kildare (*DIS* 85–6), a place that also figures in the Life of Colum of Terryglass (§13). The name assigned to his father reflects the early tribal designation *moccu Alla (Alda)*, whence Cualde (Ó Riain, *Corpus*, §§707.93, 722.22).

§2 *Mochoinne.* S has Mochonna.

§2 *Assaroe.* Text: *Tullum (gurgitem S) Ruaydh*. There was a house of Cistercian monks in Assaroe, founded as a daughter house of Boyle in 1178 (Gwynn and Hadcock, *Medieval religious houses*, 127).

§4 *a huge grave.* S locates the grave by the side of the road.

§5 *Mobhaoi.* S has the corrupt forms *Molan* and *Moban* for *Mobhaoi* in this section.

§5 *monastic town of Clonmacnoise.* M uses the word *civitas* 'city' whereas S has *coenobium*, 'monastery'. Clonmacnoise was the seat of a house of canons regular, founded about the middle of the twelfth century (Gwynn and Hadcock, *Medieval religious houses*, 165).

§5   *rule and communal custom.* Though Mobhaoi was principally associated with the relatively minor church of Cloney, Co. Kildare, he was sometimes confused with Baodán of Clonmacnoise, which might explain why his 'place' was supposed to follow a communal rule (*DIS* 86). Despite the suggestion that he may have originally represented Bréanainn of Clonfert (*VSHP* ii, 365), the reference here to rule and custom is unlikely to have any connection with Clonfert (Bhreathnach, 'Who controlled Roscrea?', 34).

§6   *the lepers washed themselves.* A similar incident, also involving cleansing of leprosy, is reported in Ruadhán's Life (§22).

§7   *to build churches.* Here, as elsewhere in the Life, the word *locus* is used for church.

§7   *in honour of the Lord.* S has 'in honour of God and his mother'.

§7   *fragrant plain.* S has *herbosus campus*, 'grassy plain', for M's *holerosus campus*. The attention paid here and in the following sections to Lusmagh suggests that Roscrea was making a case for jurisdiction over a church that later fell to Clonfert.

§8   *ate apples.* S also identifies the fruit as *poma*, 'apples'.

§9   *Díoma.* The Book of Díoma, now TCD MS 59, was apparently in Roscrea when the Life was written in the twelfth century (Gwynn and Gleeson, *A history*, 64–71; Kenney, *Sources*, §458). As the book would have been regarded as a highly prized relic, the suggestion that it was compiled in Lusmagh would have strengthened Roscrea's claim to jurisdiction over this church.

§10   *Lusmagh in ... Múscraighe Tíre.* This is inaccurate as the territory of Múscraighe Tíre comprised the baronies of Lower Ormond and Upper Ormond in Co. Tipperary, whereas Lusmagh is in the barony of Garrycastle, Co. Offaly (Cunningham, *The Anglo-Norman advance*, 22). For differing opinions as to when Lusmagh became part of the diocese of Clonfert, see ibid., 27 (n. 52).

§11   S omits this section.

§11   *church in the lands of the Leinstermen.* Mobhaoi was attached to Cloney in the parish of Kilberry, Co. Kildare: see above at §2.

§11   *you will die after a few days.* Mobhaoi's feast fell on 13 December, nominally the day of his death, which he shared with Colum of Terryglass (*MartO* 251; *MartG* 238).

§12   *Osán.* S omits this name.

§13   S omits this section.

§13   *Tara.* Why distant Tara, rather than nearby Cashel, receives mention here is unclear.

§14   *relatives.* M uses the word *cognati*, 'relatives', whereas S has *amici*, 'friends'.

§14   *River Brosna.* Mention of this river, known as the Little Brosna, gives the impression that the saint's relatives were thought to be coming from the north.

§14   *until Monday.* Travel on Sunday, and especially on solemn feastdays, was regarded by the ecclesiastical authorities as a transgression: see O'Keeffe, 'Cáin Domnaig'.

§14   *until Pentecost.* Easter to Pentecost was known in the liturgy as Paschal time, during which no fast was allowed.

§15   *a net.* Text: *ratis*. S speaks of a *cimba*, 'bell'.

§15   *River Shannon.* Lusmagh lies near the River Shannon.

§16   *hoe.* Text: *sarculum*, 'hoe'. S uses the term *sacculus*, 'small bag'.

§16   *land of Ossory ... the church called Seanros at the lake of Cré.* S does not mention Lurga and Ossory, thus making better sense since Seanros was near Roscrea. While sometimes thought to be a separate foundation, the likelihood is that Monaincha is intended. This retreat had all the characteristics of remoteness that went with Crónán's foundation. It was associated, among others, with Ealáir, a notable representative of the *céili Dé*, who died in 807. Ealáir figures, together with Maol Díthreibh of Terryglass, among those mentioned in the Rule of Tallaght (Gwynn, 'The Rule of Tallaght', 21; Follet, *Céli Dé in Ireland*, 90–2). Later, Monaincha came to be regarded as one of the 'Wonders of Ireland' and, as such, a focus of pilgrimage (Gwynn and Gleeson, *A history*, 56–60).

§16   *for a long time.* S asserts that Crónán soon after 'happily rested' there (*postmodum ... requievit*), perhaps in the sense that he was later buried there; M assigns his burial to his foundation in Roscrea.

§17   *Bishop Fursa.* Why Fursa should have been introduced to this Life, as also to the Life of Mochaomhóg (§31), is unclear; his connections with the Tipperary area were slight (*DIS* 359).

§17   *hives.* M has *mansiones*, whereas S has the more usual *alvearia*.

§17   *surplice.* The word used in the text is *subpellectilis*.

§17   *some clothes.* The word 'clothes' is lacking in the Latin text.

§17   *Roscrea.* According to his Life, Mochuda of Lismore ordered Crónán to abandon the remote place, again on the basis that the main road would be a better place on which to receive guests, before deciding with him the site of the new monastery in Roscrea (*VSHP* i, 194 §61). F.J. Byrne regarded this episode as reaction to the reforming impulse of a ninth-century ascetic who re-established the site on the island of Loch Cré, but this would hardly apply in a twelfth-century text (Byrne, 'Church and politics', 671).

§18   It has been suggested that this episode reflects the killing in 1171 of Domhnall Ua Fógarta, king of southern Éile, by Domhnall Mac Giolla Phádraig, king of Ossory (Bhreathnach, 'Who controlled Roscrea?', 34).

§18   *people ... territory.* The words *gens* and *plebs*, which are used by both M and S, are translated here as people and territory.

§18   *all ... found to be safe.* S makes an exception of one man who did not seek refuge with Crónán.

§19   *Mochaomhóg.* It has been suggested that Mochaomhóg was brought into the Life with a view to putting his church's patrons, the Uí Bhriain, in their place, but there is nothing negative in the way he is presented (Bhreathnach, 'Who controlled Roscrea?', 39). Neither Crónán nor his church figures in Mochaomhóg's Life.

§19   *a certain lay-brother.* The identification of the lay-brother as Mochaomhóg lacks textual support (Bhreathnach, 'Who controlled Roscrea?', 39).

§19   *Christ ... in a guest.* For another example of the concept of a Christ-like guest, see §23 below.

§20   *Colmán son of Miodhghna.* S omits the name of Colmán's father. A saint named Colmán son of Miodhghna, alias Colmán Cúile (*DIS* 203), who is credited with acting as tutor of Colum of Terryglass (§4), is connected with Clonkeen (Cluain Caoin) in the parish of Clonenagh, Co. Laois, but the man presented here is treated as a layman.

§20   *Ráith Eidhin.* S omits the place-name, which may refer to Rathavin in the parish of Rathcool, barony of Middlethird, Co. Tipperary (Ó Cearbhaill, *Cluain i logainmneacha*, 67). The place is likely to have been impropriate to Roscrea priory.

§21   *Colmán.* This second Colmán is left unidentified.

§21   *Ráith Fhiodhalta.* S omits the place-name, which has not been identified. Its lands were probably also impropriate to Roscrea priory.

§22   *Corca Mhoicheine.* S omits this name, which may be a variant of Corca Theine, a tribal name used for part of the territory of Éile, now represented by the parish of Templemore (Hogan, *Onomasticon*, 256; Ó Cearbhaill, *Cluain i logainmneacha*, 198).

§22 *seed of Aoldobhar.* S also omits this name. Among the leading families of Corca Theine were the Clann Mhaoil Uidhir, who are possibly intended by the text's reference to *semen Aildibuir* (O'Brien, *Corpus*, 154a38).

§23 S omits this section.

§23 *as if to Christ.* For another example of the concept of a Christ-like guest, see §19 above.

§24 *Fínghein.* According to the annals, Fínghein died in 619 (*AI*). His *ceinéal*, 'kindred', the Ceinéal Fínghein, later the Uí Shúilleabháin, appear to have occupied lands north of Cashel in the area about Derrynaflan (parish of Graystown).

§24 *a fort called Ráith Bheagáin.* The word *villa* (in both M and S) is here taken to mean 'fort'. Ráith Bheagáin may be used here, as in the Life of Abán, for the prebend of Kilbrickane in the deanery of Eliogarty (*VSHP* i, 18; Ó Cearbhaill, *Cill i logainmneacha*, 68; idem, *Cluain i logainmneacha*, 47).

§24 *region of Midhe.* The territory of Midhe originally comprised the present county of Westmeath but later extended into the county of Meath.

§24 *lake of Cré.* This lake, Irish Loch Cré, is at Monaincha in the parish of Corbally, a few miles from Roscrea.

§25 *Maonach.* According to the annals, Maonach son of Fínghein, king of Munster, died in 662 (*AI*). *Maon*, whence Maonach, has the meaning 'dumb'.

§26 *gospel-book.* Cainneach of Aghaboe is said to have copied a gospel-book at Monaincha (*DIS* 139).

§26 *island on the lake.* The island referred to here is Monaincha.

§26 *Crónán's monastery.* At this point, S ends, but there is no obvious loss of manuscript.

§27 *Cluain Earc.* This place has not been identified (Ó Riain, Ó Murchadha and Murray, *Historical dictionary*, v, 113).

§29 *28 April.* The text refers to 'the fourth calends of May'.

LIFE OF MOCHAOMHÓG OF LEIGH

§1 *race of Conmhaicne.* A full pedigree of the saint, in general agreement with that of the corpus of saints' genealogies (Ó Riain, *Corpus*, §362), is added in the lower margin of M.

§1   *His father abandoned his home place.* A much abbreviated version of the circumstances surrounding the arrival of Mochaomhóg's father in Munster, his beheading in battle, miraculous resuscitation and subsequent birth of his son is contained in Íde's Life (*VSHP* ii, 121–2 §xviii).

§1   *Corca Oiche.* Rendered *Corcoiche* in the Irish Life, this is mistakenly given as *Corca Baysce* in the Latin text. Uí Chonaill Ghabhra was in west Limerick, mainly in the baronies of Connello Upper and Lower; it formed the western part of Uí Fhidhgheinte, the eastern part of which was formed by Uí Chairbre. Molua son of Oiche, who is depicted below (§§10, 29) as one of Mochaomhóg's companions, is said to have belonged to the Corca Oiche (*VSHP* ii, 206 §1).

§1   *people of the Déise.* The Déise had settlements not only in Waterford, where the barony of Decies still recalls them, but also in east Limerick in the barony of Small County (earlier An Déis Bheag).

§1   *Neas.* Neas may be the lady of that name who is described in the tract on the mothers of the saints as mother of the priest Caomhán (Ó Riain, *Corpus*, §722.48). Describing him as king of the Déise, the Irish Life gives the name Faolán to Neas's father, but this is probably in error for Ceann Faoladh, the name usually given to Íde's father (Ó Riain, *Corpus*, §93).

§1   *Íde.* This saint's main church was at Killeedy in the barony of Glenquin, but a second church, named Kilmeedy, lay within the barony of Connello, which took its name from Uí Chonaill Ghabhra.

§3   *Crunnmhaol.* Crunnmhaol son of Aodh of the Uí Chairbre is probably intended (O'Brien, *Corpus*, 152a21, 154c47). He died as king of Uí Fhidhgheinte in 649. Among his descendants were the Uí Dhonnabháin (Pender, 'The O Clery book', §2034) who, following great warfare between north and south Munster in 1177, moved away from south Limerick, eventually settling in the part of Corca Laoighdhe in south-west Cork that went on to bear their 'tribal' name of Uí Chairbre, anglicized Carbery (Ó Murchadha, *Family names*, 124). Their presence there may also have contributed to the connection established below (§4) between Fachtna of Ross Carbery and Íde.

§3   *Corca Oiche.* M again has *Corco Baysce* as against Br's more correct *Corco Che*.

§4   *Fachtna.* M has *Fachnanus*. Fachtna was venerated as founder-patron of Ross Carbery in south-west Cork (*DIS* 300–1). Nearby, at Abbeymahon, was a house of Cistercian monks.

§4   *group of scholars.* This is in line with the triad that places 'Ireland's learning' in Ross Carbery (Meyer, *The Triads*, 2 §17).

§4   *five days.* This seems an inordinately long time for a journey by foot between Ross Carbery and south Limerick, roughly a distance of fifty-five miles.

§4   *Corca Oiche.* As above, M has *Corco Basce* here as against Br's *Corcoiche.*

§5   *This wagon is making noise under a king.* A similar motif is recorded in the Life of Comhghall of Bangor (*VSHH* 332, 406), Mochaomhóg's later mentor (§8).

§6   *Caoimhghin.* Br has *caomh tsean*, 'beautiful [and] old', which is more in line with Íde's comment. In Ó Riain, *Corpus*, §722.48, the saint's non-hypocoristic name is rendered Caomhán. Mochaomhóg does not mean 'my beautiful youth'; it is a pet form of Caomh, alias Caomhán. The Latin form *Pulcherius*, 'beautiful', is sometimes used of the saint.

§7   *globe of fire.* See also the note to Colum's Life at p. 86 above.

§7   *Holy Ghost.* The Holy Ghost is regularly associated with fire, as can be seen from the Gospel of St Matthew (3.11) and the Acts of the Apostles (2.2–4).

§8   *Comhghall.* For Comhghall, see *DIS* 217–19.

§8   *five disciples.* Why Mochaomhóg should already have disciples is not explained.

§8   *before long.* Latin *non post plurimos dies*, 'after not many days'.

§9   *Rademan.* Text: *Ráith Deamáin*; Br reads *Ráith Emhna.* As Reeves (*Ecclesiastical antiquities*, 216) points out, there was formerly a castle in Rademan, parish of Kilmore, barony of Kinelarty, Co. Down. The Mic Artáin (McArtans) were chiefs of this area, which is about twenty miles from Bangor.

§9   *three thousand monks.* The number of monks at Bangor is elsewhere variously numbered four and forty thousand (Plummer, *Irish litanies*, 60–1n.).

§10   *where he will point out to you.* M has *ubi ipse tibi annuerit*, whereas Br reads: *go mbeitheá ag foghnamh dó*, 'where you might serve him'.

§10   *Laichtín ... Luchtighearn.* Br's version, which omits Luchtighearn, is a little confused at this point. For a discussion of the passage, see pp 42–3 above.

§11   *Anatrim.* This is in the parish of Offerlane, barony of Upperwoods, Co. Laois. The story of its choice as a site is also the subject of an episode in the Life of Colum of Terryglass (§§13–14), which describes how Caomhán, Colum's disciple, is shown where his church will lie by a previously mute herd. For an account of this saint, who shared his name with Mochaomhóg, see *DIS* 155.

§11   *Brónach.* Br reads *Senbhrónach* for this man who is not known from any other source. It may be noted, however, that a branch of Fothairt, whose settlements were scattered throughout Leinster, was known as Uí Bhrónaigh (Ó Muraíle, *The great book*, 366.3).

§11 *Caomhán*: see note above at §6.

§12 *Éile*. This territory was divided into two parts, northern and southern, corresponding to the present Offaly baronies of Clonlisk and Ballybritt and the Tipperary baronies of Ikerrin and Eliogarty. Southern Éile was ruled by the Uí Fhógarta (whence Eliogarty) and northern Éile by the Uí Chearbhaill. Northern Éile is intended here. For the varying extent of Éile, see Cunningham, *The Anglo-Norman advance*, 13–23.

§12 *Clonmore*. This may refer to Clonmore in the parish of Seirkieran, which lay within Ballybritt and thus within the territory of Éile (Ó Riain, Ó Murchadha and Murray, *Historical dictionary*, v, 141).

§12 *Caomhán*. This man, more correctly Cnáimhín, son of Maonach, was the grandfather of Cearbhall, *a quo* Uí Chearbhaill (O'Brien, *Corpus*, 154a35: *v.l.* BB Cnáimhín). He died in 903, according to the Annals of the Four Masters, and this is a good example of how little chronological consideration influenced the choice of representative persons in Lives of saints.

§12 *Rathenny*. Text: *Raith Eanaidh*; Rathenny is in the parish of Cullenwaine, barony of Clonlisk, Co. Offaly. The site is about ten miles from the Clonmore mentioned above: see Cunningham, *The Anglo-Norman advance*, 36.

§13 *the ruler*. Neither the ruler nor his place of residence is named, but Mochaomhóg's church of Leigh (Liath Mochaomhóg) lay within the barony of Eliogarty, in other words in southern Éile of the Uí Fhógarta.

§13 *soothsayer*. M reads *magus*. Br omits this passage.

§13 *the lake of Lurga*. See also the Life of Crónán (§16) and the Life of Ruadhán (§25) for episodes involving churches near this lake.

§13 *boundaries*. The term used in the text is *termini*, which gives Irish *tearmonn*, 'area of sanctuary'.

§13 *his swineherd*. Swineherds are frequently involved in the choice of church-sites, and nowhere more notably than in the story of what is regarded as Ireland's earliest Christian foundation, at Saul in Co. Down, the home of a swineherd (Mulchrone, *Bethu Phátraic*, 376–85; Stokes, *The tripartite Life*, 36).

§14 *bell will be mute*. For other examples of a previously mute bell ringing on arrival at the site of a church, see *VSHP* i, clxxvii (n. 5).

§14 *very grey, wild … boar*. The presence of a wild animal at the site of a future church is a common motif, but the animal's colour rarely has a bearing on the name of the site (Jankulak, 'Alba longa in the Celtic regions', 280). For another Tipperary example of the presence of a wild animal, see the Life of Ruadhán §3.

§14 *the name Liath.* Liath, gen. Léith, is a common enough element in Irish place-names (Hogan, *Onomasticon*, 488–9).

§14 *a three-day fast.* This length of fast commonly formed part of the ceremony surrounding the consecration of a new church: see note above to Life of Colum (§8).

§15 *Colmán son of Dáire.* Colmán was patron of Doire Mór, now Longfordpass church in the parish of Kilcooly, barony of Eliogarty: see *DIS* 195–6; Manning, 'Daire Mór'.

§15 *Eoghanacht.* Under a variant form of his pedigree, Colmán was considered a son of Aonghas son of Nadh Fraoich, Eoghanacht king of Cashel (Ó Riain, *Corpus*, §191; Walsh, *Genealogiae*, 116).

§15 *I shall go to the ... bishop.* Visiting a person betokened homage (Ó Riain, *The making of a saint*, 54–5). Here, therefore, Mochaomhóg pays homage to Colmán.

§15 *the fraternity between them.* The primary purpose of fraternities in the Middle Ages was to secure mutual support in death through masses and prayers. They also provided a forum for the resolving of disputes (Cross and Livingstone, *The Oxford dictionary*, 637). Many medieval fraternity books survive on the Continent.

§15 *Íde had foretold.* See also above at §14.

§16 *Rónán son of Bleidhín.* Rónán is nowhere to be found in the genealogies, but his father Bleidhín is included in a southern Éile pedigree that traces his descent to Eochu Feidhleach son of [Feidhlimidh] Reachtaidh, usually the progenitor of the Fothairt group of families (O'Brien, *Corpus*, 325c43; Ó Muraíle, *The great book*, 367.6).

§16 *chanting terce.* Traditionally, terce and nones were sung at the third and ninth hours, whence their names.

§17 *sensual pleasures.* Br omits the reference to sensual pleasure.

§17 *Finnian.* Finnian of Clonard, Co. Meath, is probably intended, but Br has *Finan*, possibly with Fíonán Cam, patron of Kinnity, Co. Offaly, in mind (*DIS* 319–21, 327–30).

§18 *Suibhne son of Diarmuid.* In the southern Éile pedigree, Suibhne son of Diarmuid is taken to have been Bleidhín's grandson (O'Brien, *Corpus*, 325c41).

§18 *Faolán son of Rónán.* Like his father Rónán, Faolán is otherwise unknown. Br reads *Feidhlim[idh]*, but he is likewise unknown.

§18   *Sléibhín*. This name is not in the southern Éile pedigree, which has Flann son of Suibhne (O'Brien, *Corpus*, 325a40).

§18   *Cainneach*. The patron of Aghaboe and Kilkenny is doubtless intended. Among the many churches associated with him was Monaincha, near Roscrea, where he is said to have copied a gospel-book (*DIS* 139).

§18   *bury among your monks*. Burial practices appear to have been a concern at the time of writing.

§18   *fort on a certain island ... in the middle of the River Suir*. The fort has not been identified. At Golden village, the Suir divides to form an island containing the remains of a keep, but this may be too far south to be intended here.

§19   *Fáilbhe Flann*. This king of Munster died, according to the annals, in 639 (*AI*).

§19   *angrily argued with one another*. What follows is reminiscent of the altercation between Ruadhán and Diarmuid, king of Tara, with its alternating curses, as is recorded in Ruadhán's Life (§17). This tussle was also accompanied by a vision seen by the king.

§20   *namely Feimhean and Mossadh*. Eugene O'Curry used this passage to discuss in great detail the relative positions of the plains of Feimhean, which comprised the area between Cashel and Clonmel (*ATigIndex* 143), and Mossadh, which extended northwards from Cashel into the territory of Éile (O'Curry, *Manuscript materials*, 485–6). The placing of Patrick in the southern plain may have been influenced by the dedications to him at Cashel itself and at St Patrick's Well near Clonmel.

§21   *Fáilbhe ... offended*. M reads *offendit*; whereas Br reads *do chuir ... tec[h]ta ar ceann*, 'sent messengers to'.

§21   *of the same race*. According to the genealogies, both men belonged to the Eoghanacht of Cashel, but were separated by several generations (Ó Riain, *Corpus*, §191; O'Brien, *Corpus*, 154c14–32).

§21   *weeds*. M reads *loliorum* and Br reads *na locht*, 'faults'.

§22   *western*. Text: *ad occidentalem*; Br reads *thoir*, 'eastern'.

§23   *in the field*. M reads *in rure* from *rus*, 'countryside'.

§25   *Cainneach ... Aghaboe*. Until Kilkenny became the principal church associated with Cainneach, Aghaboe enjoyed this status.

§25   *a journey between ... Leigh and Aghaboe lasts a full day*. The two churches are approximately twenty miles apart.

§25 *Sing for us.* Br attributes the request to Cainneach and the refusal to Mochaomhóg.

§25 *a stream of blood.* For another example of blood streaming from bread, see the Life of Ruadhán (§21).

§26 *Daghán.* For this saint, see *DIS* 251. Ennereilly was later impropriate to St Augustine's Abbey, near Bristol (White, *Extents*, 208; In(v)erollyn). Br adds Daghán's pedigree, which (slightly edited) reads: *Daghán mac Colmadhain mheic Conaill mheic Éanáin mheic Shinill mheic Conaill mheic Catháir mheic Airmora mheic Nastair mheic Fhothaidh mheic [Eachach] Láimhdheirg mheic Meisin Corb mheic Con Corb etc.*; cf. Ó Riain, *Corpus*, §256. Also added is: *Agus an lá roimh fhéil na croiche isin fhoghmhar lá an Dagháin sin*, 'and the day before the feast of the Cross in autumn is Daghán's day', i.e. 13 September.

§27 *with his companion.* The companion is not named.

§28 *Fearadhach.* M reads *Feraidhe*, Br *Fearadhaigh*. Fearadhach son of Duach, king of Ossory, who died in 583/4 (*AU*), may be intended, but no son of his is recorded.

§28 *Fíonán.* The name of the fugitive is omitted by Br.

§28 *Fachtna.* Br appears to read *Crónán*. Mention of Fachtna recalls the close connection thought to have existed between Ossory and Ross, of which the saint was patron (Ó Riain, *The making of a saint*, 84–7). Several close relatives of the saint were venerated in Ossory and Tifeaghna in the parish of Sheffin was dedicated to him, albeit under the guise of Fiachna.

§28 *you will reign.* Br allows him four years only.

§29 *Mochoime.* This saint was patron of Grangemacomb in the barony of Fassadinin, Co. Kilkenny, which was impropriate to Jerpoint Abbey (Carrigan, *The history and antiquities*, ii, 322).

§29 *Molua ... and Mofheaca.* Though principally patron of Kyle in Co. Offaly, Molua was also patron of Killaloe in Co. Kilkenny. Mofheaca, a pet form of Féichín, was patron of Sheffin, not far from Grangemacomb (Carrigan, *The history and antiquities*, ii, 326–7). Féichín's principal church at Fore in Co. Westmeath became the site of a Benedictine abbey.

§29 *roofless.* The text reads *nudus*, 'naked, bare'.

§29 *five small stones.* There would appear to be no remains of this kind at Grangemacomb (Carrigan, *The history and antiquities*, ii, 322).

§30 *Uí Aonghusa ... of the Déise.* Br reads *iarla Engusa*, 'Earl Aonghas'. For the Uí Aonghusa branch of the Déise, see O'Brien, *Corpus*, 328d9.

§30   *Faolán son of Eacha*. This man does not appear to be recorded elsewhere. Br reads: *Feidhlimthe mac Eachach*.

§30   *Cuimín Fada*. Like Mochaomhóg, this saint is reputed to have been raised at Íde's church in Killeedy (*DIS* 243–5).

§30   *cursing the lake*. Br asserts that the castle was swallowed up.

§31   *Bishop Fursa*. Why Fursa should have been introduced to this Life, and to that of Crónán (§17), is unclear; his connections with Tipperary and Kilkenny are very slight. Hamann ('St Fursa', 178) mistakenly takes Fursa to be intended by the reference to the clearly distinct archbishop of Emly.

§31   *Cuán*. Br reads *Cuana*, but the man is otherwise unknown.

§31   *Scanlán son of Faolán*. Br omits here the name of Scanlán's father but adds it at the end of the section. Though no such Scanlán is known from either annals or genealogies, his father Faolán may refer to the treacherously slain son of Eacha of the Déise, mentioned above at §30.

§31   *archbishop ... of Emly*: see above.

§31   *Cua*. M reads *Guach*, Br *Cua*. Sliabh gCua refers to the Knockmealdown Mountains.

§32   *Díoma ... son of Féichín*. For the father's name, M reads *Foethanus*, Br *Feichin*. The chieftain is otherwise unknown.

§32   *Inishlounaght*. Br reads *Inis Leamhlachta*. Inishlounaght on the River Suir – near Clonmel and at some distance from where the Nore flows into an estuary – became the site of a Cistercian abbey in 1147 (Gwynn and Hadcock, *Medieval religious houses*, 135).

§33   *plain of Munster*. Emly's location on the plain of Munster is omitted by Br.

§33   *Cuán Cearr*. The founder of Clashmore (Glais Mhór), near Lismore, is usually named Crónán; both Crónán and Cuán yield a hypocoristic form Mochua (*DIS* 233; Colgan, *Acta sanctorum*, 598.40).

§33   *the archbishop*. This is the second mention of an archbishop of Emly (cf. §31). Here, however, Br has *espoc*, 'bishop'.

§34   *Cainnear*. Colgan (*Acta sanctorum*, 598.42) thought this bearer of the name might be Cainnear daughter of Fiontan of Clooncaura, Co. Limerick, whom Molua of Kyle cured of muteness (*DIS* 141).

§35   *his churches*. M reads *loca*, 'places'.

§35   *13 March*. The text reads: 'third of the Ides of March'.

§35 Br's version of the final section is quite different from the Latin text; it refers in the usual way to many churches founded by the saint, to the many miracles performed by him and to the angels and archangels who accompanied him on his journey to heaven. It ends with a personal appeal for salvation. Attached to Br is a colophon by Mícheál Ó Cléirigh which says that part of the text was first copied in Clonmel friary from a manuscript owned by Tomás son of Éamonn Buitléir, lord of Caher, and the other part from the (same?) vellum manuscript in the Wexford friary, before being finally written up in the convent of the Donegal friars in December 1629.

LIFE OF RUADHÁN OF LORRHA

§1 *Eoghanacht.* S assigns Ruadhán to the Dubhraighe branch of the Uí Dhuach, who occupied the barony of Fassadinin and parts of the adjoining baronies (Crannagh, Galmoy, Clarmallagh) in Kilkenny and Laois (*ATigIndex* 192). Ruadhán gave name to Tullaroan (*Tulach Ruadháin*) in the barony of Crannagh. The Eoghanacht descent accorded him here is in keeping with the saint's 'official' pedigree (Ó Riain, *Corpus*, §208). The vernacular version of the Life (Br) gives a fuller version of the pedigree in line with the Ormond recension of the corpus of saints' genealogies.

§1 *Byrra (Birri).* This reflects the more usual Bearn, as found in Ó Riain, *Corpus*, §208. Dál mBirn (genitive of Bearn) was used to refer to the people of Ossory. Br gives his father's name as Fearghas Beirn.

§1 *Uí Dhuach.* The affiliation of the Uí Dhuach to the Eoghanachta is confirmed in O'Brien, *Corpus*, 148a50.

§1 *Clonard.* Br places Clonard in Uí Néill an Deiscirt, 'Southern Uí Néill'. In the Salamancan version (§§1, 11), Finnian is twice described as a bishop, a rank that would first have become appropriate in the twelfth century, after the establishment of the see of Clonard.

§1 *having found a site.* S places Ruadhán's first foundation among the Maca Neachtain, another name for Neachtraighe, one of whose branches was associated with Uaithne (now Owney, as in the name of the barony of Owney and Arra, adjoining the territory of Múscraighe Tíre; Ó Cíobháin, 'The toponymy', 81). Br adds 'Ara Mac Ua Neitt', an alternative name for Araidh Tíre in north-west Tipperary, to Múscraighe (Ó Riain, Ó Murchadha and Murray, *Historical dictionary*, i, 76). Kilruane (from Ceall Ruadháin) in the barony of Lower Ormond (formerly Múscraighe) takes its name from Ruadhán.

§2   *Lorrha.* Br adds *i nUrmumain*, 'in Ormond'.

§3   *a wild boar.* According to S and Br, the boar abandoned a hollow in a tree (*ex concavo ligno; i ccúas croind*). The presence of a wild animal on the site chosen for a church is a common topos (*VSHP* i, cxliv). See also the Life of Crónán (§14).

§4   *Bréanainn … Tulach Bhréanainn.* S and Br add the tribal designation Maca Alta (alias Alltraighe) to Bréanainn's name. Although apparently near Lorrha, the *tulach*, 'hillock', has yet to be identified.

§4   *Clonfert.* Br renders the name as 'Cluain Ferta Brenaind', while S attributes to Ruadhán the prophecy that Clonfert will not be weaker (*infirmior*) than Lorrha.

§5   *a large parochia.* S also asserts that Ruadhán acquired a large *parochia*.

§7   *Slanore … in Cairbre Mhór.* This place, Irish Snámh Luthair, is in the parish of Kilmore, Co. Cavan. A place named Tullyroane in the parish of Annagh, not far from Kilmore, may take its name from Ruadhán (logainm.ie: 'Tullyroane'). Cairbre Mhór comprised almost the whole of Co. Longford and may have extended into Co. Cavan (Ó Riain, Ó Murchadha and Murray, *Historical dictionary*, iii, 8–9). At Lough Oughter, near Slanore, there was a house of Premonstratensian canons regular, founded as a daughter-house of Holy Trinity on Lough Key (Gwynn and Hadcock, *Medieval religious houses*, 206; cf. §9 below).

§8   *Ros Éinne in … Oirthir.* M has *Ross Ernem*, Br *Ros Eirnine*, and S *Roys Enni*. The site has yet to be confidently identified but, as *Oirthir* (later baronies of Lower Orior and Upper Orior) included most of Co. Armagh, the place may now be represented by Crossnenagh in the parish of Keady, six miles from Armagh city. Among the townlands of this parish is Ruan (from Ruadhán), possibly representing the saint. A place called Tullyroan in the Armagh parish of Clonfeacle may also take its name from the saint (logainm.ie: 'Tullyroan').

§8   *fort.* The Latin word used here by M is *villa*, whereas S and Br have *civitas* and *cathair*.

§8   *for a long time.* S, Br and R refer here to a time of pestilence.

§8   *blessed … and prayed.* According to S, Br and R, the saint was ringing his bell as he went around.

§8   *The people then gave thanks.* According to Br, the people also took off their clothes, presumably to present them as payment to the saint.

§9   *south of Ireland.* The saint was in fact moving west into Connacht. S does not specify the direction, whereas R and Br omit this section.

§9 *Dairí*. Though there is no other record of Ruadhán having a sister named Dairí (*Dare* M, *Daroi* S), a female saint of this name was well known in Connacht, in Tirawley (Co. Mayo) and at churches named Kildaree in Co. Galway (see *DIS* 254). The sisters otherwise recorded for the saint were named Caol and Ruadhnaid (§15).

§9 *Uí Oilealla*. M has *In finibus Hilela*, S *in finibus nepotum Ailella*. This place gave name to the barony of Tirerrill, Co. Sligo, within which was located the church of Shancough, a site more usually associated with Ailbhe (*DIS* 60). Shancough (Seanchua) was impropriate to the Premonstratensian canons of Lough Key, who established a daughter-house at Lough Oughter in Co. Cavan (Gwynn and Hadcock, *Medieval religious houses*, 205; Freeman, *The compossicion booke*, 129, 154; see §7 above).

§10 *cattle-shed*. M reads *a fetu*, but S reads *a bocceto*, 'from the cattle-shed', which is the reading adopted here.

§10 *wickedness of the servant*. Br uses the term *domiad*, 'discourtesy', towards guests, thus agreeing with S, which reads *non erat curialis hospitibus*, 'he was not courteous to guests'.

§10 *a nearby lake*. Friars Lough, a little west of Lorrha, may be intended.

§11 *Araidh Chliach*. This people and its territory were located in east Limerick. S and Br omit the reference to Munster.

§12 *nobleman*. S describes this man as a king (*rex*) and, together with Br, his wife as a queen (*regina*).

§12 *Cuala*. this refers to a territory in south Dublin and north Wicklow.

§12 *a certain youth*. S identifies this youth as the one whose hands had been blessed by Ruadhán in the previous section.

§12 *assist the noble lady*. S, Br and R assert that the youth was ordered to bless the water, and then spit into it before giving it to the lady.

§12 *linen cloth*. In S, Br and R, this is described as the king's linen cloth, with Br taking '*Leuia* (*leini* St)' to be the name of the cloth.

§13 *Shannon Estuary*. This is described in the text as the sea of Limerick. Bréanainn is reputed to have founded 'a famous monastery' on the island of Inis Dá Dhroma (Inishdadroum) in the Shannon Estuary (*DIS* 116). Nearby, and in the same parish of Killadysert, is Canon Island, which takes its name from a priory of the Augustinian canons (Gwynn and Hadcock, *Medieval religious houses*, 162).

§13 *Ruadhán's staff*. S and Br have *cucullus* (*cochall*), 'cowl', in place of staff.

§14 *There were … monastery of Lorrha.* Much the same details, with some variants, are provided by the Salamancan version of the Life of Finnian (*VSHH* 103–4 §§24–6).

§14 *fifty monks.* S, R and Br have 150 monks. Finnian's Life does not give the number (*VSHH* 103 §24).

§14 *a certain tree.* Finnian's Life (*VSHH* 103 §24) describes it as a *tylia*, 'lime-tree', the same term as is used by the biographer of Colum of Terryglass for the tree that sated the saint and his companions (§16). It also asserts that the sap of the tree filled a vessel between sunset and noon on the following day, whereas it only half-filled a vessel in between.

§14 *Finnian.* Br adds: 'Some say that he was master of all the saints of Ireland'. Br and Finnian's Life (*VSHH* 103 §25) add that he was accompanied by the saints of Ireland.

§14 *Ruadhán's permission.* Finnian's Life, S, R and Br omit the reference to permission.

§14 *eat and drink tonight.* According to S and Br, there was now enough sap for the monks only and none for guests.

§14 *little river.* Finnian's Life (*VSHH* 103 §25), S and Br assert that the water was being drawn from the well.

§14 *its trace remains.* This is not stated in Finnian's Life (*VSHH* 103 §25).

§14 *gave thanks to God.* S says that those who drank the wine became inebriated.

§14 *Pray to God.* S and Br have *arate* (*oirfither*), 'plough' for M's *orate*, 'pray'. Finnian's Life adds that, should part of the land be manured following his blessing, it would produce nothing but herbs and a few ears of corn (*VSHH* 103 §26).

§14 *Finnian went back.* S and Br agree in stating that Finnian blessed Ruadhán's place and land.

§§15–16 The tale of the encounter between Ruadhán and Diarmuid, king of Tara, also survives in vernacular versions. One version, Diarmuid's death-tale, 'Aided Diarmada meic Fergusa cerrbeoil' (ADFC), is close to the account given here (O'Grady, *Silva gadelica*, i, 75–8). The other version, entitled 'Stair ar Aed baclámh' (SAB), adds a good deal of incidental detail (O'Grady, *Silva gadelica*, i, 66–71). An extensive account is also provided by the Annals of Clonmacnoise (*AClon.* 85–8).

§15 *Cearbhall.* Br gives the alternative form 'Fearghas Ceirbheól'.

§15   *herald.* In S, the herald is named Bacc Lom; in Br Bacclámh and in R Becc
Lomyn. Describing him as a *giolla gaoi*, 'spear-servant', SAB names him Aodh
Baclámh. *AClon.*, which refers to the steward as 'sargiant', calls him 'Backlaure',
apparently in error for 'Backlaue' (Baclámh).

§15   *Seanach.* This was one of the 'elder saints' of the Múscraighe (*DIS* 555–6).
There is no record of his mother's name; nor is he elsewhere associated either
with Aodh or with Ruadhán's sisters, who are otherwise absent from the saint's
record. SAB calls him Seanán. *AClon.* substitutes Ruadhán for Seanach.

§15   *Aodh.* Aodh Guaire was his name according to S, R, Br, SAB, ADFC and *AClon.*

§15   *not wishing.* M has *ualens* in error for *volens*, 'wishing'.

§15   *flight to Britain.* S, R and Br assert that Ruadhán accompanied Aodh to Britain.
AClon. takes Britain to mean 'Wales'.

§15   *king of Britain.* R and Br add a reference to the nobles of that country.

§15   *to ensure that Aodh.* M has *Aedhanus* here in place of *Aidus.*

§15   *many churches.* The word *loca*, literally 'places', in M is translated here as 'churches'.

§15   *Pollrone.* From Poll Ruadháin, this is in the barony of Iverk, Co. Kilkenny. As
with several other sites mentioned in the Life, Pollrone was not only named
after Ruadhán, it was also associated with Augustinians, in this case the Arroasian
canonesses of Kilculliheen, founded in 1151 (Gwynn and Hadcock, *Medieval
religious houses*, 319). Pollrone was impropriate to the canonesses (Carrigan,
The history and antiquities, iv, 149). SAB asserts that Poll Ruadháin was named
from the cave in which Aodh Guaire was hidden.

§15   *underneath you.* In S, this is rendered *sub sede tua*, 'under your seat'.

§15   *lit a torch.* In S, the lit torch was allegedly in the hand of a servant on his way
to Aodh.

§15   *Donnán.* There is no other mention of a Donnán in association with Pollrone.

§16   *accompanied by Bréanainn.* This is the second mention in the text of Bréanainn,
whose church at Clonfert also became the site of a house of canons regular.
Charles Plummer originally put forward (*VSHP* 247n.) but later qualified
(*BNÉ* ii, 363) his view that the Clonfert saint was probably intended here. Br,
SAB and ADFC add Biorra (Birr), and SAB includes 'the twelve apostles of
Ireland' among those who accompanied the saints, before going on to state that,
although then on his voyage, Brendan of Clonfert, having been advised by an
angel of the turn of events, hastened back to join the others. Neither S nor R
mention Bréanainn. Cf. §4 above.

§16 *sang while fasting*. The words used by M are *canebant ieiuni*, whereas S has *psalmos ... canebat*, 'he sang psalms'. However, it is asserted in the next section (§17) that the saints fasted against the king.

§17 *The saints ... firm in faith*. This opening passage is omitted in S, R and Br.

§17 *the king ... had a dream*. In SAB the dream, described in verse, is attributed to Diarmuid's wife Mughain. The king's interpretation of the dream is omitted from S and Br.

§17 *holding vigil*. Br adds that it was taboo for the king to remain beyond sunrise in Tara.

§18 *out of the sea*. According to S and Br, the horses emerged from the sea near Pollrone. According to SAB, they were made out of seals.

§18 *swift horses*. S and Br remark that they surpassed other horses in racing.

§20 *the tree ... immediately rose up*. For a similar response to a saint's command, see Mochaomhóg's Life (§22).

§21 *arrival of ... guests*. S, R and Br place this occurrence during Lent.

§21 *bread ... as raw and bloody meat*. For another example of this, see Mochaomhóg's Life (§25).

§22 *his staff upon the ground*. For a list of other examples of this motif, see Bray, 'The study of folk-motif', 272.

§22 *pond ... by Ruadhán's name*. In S, the name is rendered Piscina Ruodani; in Br §16, this becomes 'Pisina', later called 'topar Ruadhain'. A well called after Ruadhán, near a stone (*leac*) likewise bearing his name in the saint's graveyard at Lorrha, is mentioned in a note to martyrologies at 3 September; its water was allegedly once changed to wine by Colmán of Kilclonfert (*MartO* 198; *MartT* 116).

§23 This section is omitted in Br.

§23 *fire*. For several other examples of fire that does no harm, see *VSHP* i, cxxxviii (n. 6).

§24 *Colmán Eala*. This saint was patron of Lynally, Co. Offaly. As Laisréan of Durrow is supposed to have assisted Colmán in marking out the boundary of his church, it may be assumed that it was impropriate to Durrow, the site of a house of canons regular (*DIS* 204).

§25 *Doire Eidhneach*. This church, whose patrons were two saints named Flann, is now known as Derrynaflan; it is in the parish of Graystown (*DIS* 344–5).

§25 *Colmán son of Daráine ... Longfordpass.* Longfordpass (Doire Mór) is in the parish of Kilcooly, Co. Tipperary. Colmán was its patron (*DIS* 195–6).

§25 *Fear Domhain.* There is no mention of the beast or of the hero who cut him in two in S, R or Br; nor is Fear Domhain known from any other source.

§26 *in a certain place.* This place is identified as Araidh in S and Br; one section of Araidh, known as Araidh Tíre, was located in north-west Tipperary (Ó Riain, Ó Murchadha and Murray, *Historical dictionary*, i, 76). St adds, probably erroneously, 'Cliach' to Araidh, which would place it in east Limerick.

§27 *region of Uí Luighdheach.* This region, omitted in Br, gave name to 'Ileagh' in the barony of Eliogarty (Éile Uí Fhógarta), Co. Tipperary, and Borrisoleigh (Buirgheas Ua Luighdheach) in the parish of Glenkeen.

§28 *Tullaroan.* Text: *Tulach Ruadháin.* The reference is probably to Tullaroan in the Kilkenny barony of Crannagh, which borders on the barony of Ikerrin, formerly part of the kingdom of south Éile in Tipperary.

§29 A similar story is told in the Life of Cainneach, which describes how he, accompanied by Colum Cille and Comhghall, hastened to the aid of Eoghan of Ardstraw in his aerial struggle against demons, during which Colum dropped his *graffium*, 'stilus'.

§29 *Éighmheach.* S and Br preface the name with Odo/Aodh but no other mention of Aodh Éighmheach is preserved. The attempt by one vernacular version of the Life to rationalize it as the legendary Aodh Eangach is hardly correct (*BNÉ* i, 327n; cf. O'Brien, *Corpus*, 439).

§29 *church for God.* Aodh's churches in Midhe were located at Rahugh and Killare.

§29 *down from the sky.* M has *caelum*, whereas S has *in celesti regno*, 'in the heavenly kingdom'.

§29 *writing-board.* S and Br maintain that Colum Cille forgetfully left it in Ruadhán's hand.

§29 *Baoithín.* S renders the name as *Bithín(us)*.

§30 *After this ... passing.* This sentence is omitted by S and Br.

§30 *15 April.* This is expressed in the text as 'the seventeenth calends of May'. The date of the saint's death and the continuing miracles are omitted by S and Br.

§30 *Amen.* Br adds an account of the relationship between Ruadhán and the Uí Shúilleabháin (O'Sullivans), the name of whose church of Kilnaruane, near Bantry, may derive from the name of the saint.

Bibliography

Anderson, A.O. and M.O. Anderson (eds), *Adomnán's Life of Columba* (London and Edinburgh, 1961; rev. ed. Oxford, 1991).

Bhreathnach, E., 'The genealogies of Leinster as a source for local cults' in J. Carey, M. Herbert and P. Ó Riain (eds), *Studies in Irish hagiography: saints and scholars* (Dublin, 2001), 250–67.

Bhreathnach, E., 'Who controlled Roscrea in the twelfth century?' in P. Harbison and V. Hall (eds), *A carnival of learning* (Roscrea, 2012), 33–40.

Bieler, L. (ed.), *The Patrician texts in the Book of Armagh* (Dublin, 1979).

Boyle, E., 'Echtgus Úa Cúanáin's poetic treatise on the Eucharist' in J. Mullins, J. Ní Ghrádaigh and R. Hawtree (eds), *Envisioning Christ on the cross: Ireland and the early medieval West* (Dublin, 2013), 181–94.

Bray, D.A., 'The study of folk-motifs in early Irish hagiography: problems of approach and rewards at hand' in J. Carey, M. Herbert and P. Ó Riain (eds), *Studies in Irish hagiography: saints and scholars* (Dublin, 2001), 268–77.

Breen, M. and R. Ua Cróinín, 'Some tower houses of east Corca Bhaiscinn and the Shannon Estuary', pt 2, *The Other Clare*, 37 (2013), 5–11.

Byrne, F.J., 'Church and politics, *c*.750–*c*.1100' in D. Ó Cróinín (ed.), *A new history of Ireland, i: Prehistoric and early Ireland* (Oxford, 2005).

Byrne, F.J., *Irish kings and high-kings* (London, 1973; repr. with add. notes and corrigenda, Dublin, 2001).

Carney, J., 'A Maccucáin, Sruith in Tíag', *Celtica*, 15 (1983), 25–41.

Carrigan, W., *The history and antiquities of the diocese of Ossory*, 4 vols (Dublin, 1905; repr. Kilkenny, 1981).

Colgan, J. (ed.), *Acta sanctorum veteris et majoris Scotiae seu Hiberniae ... sanctorum insulae*, i (Louvain, 1645; repr. Dublin, 1947).

Colgrave, B. and R.A.B. Mynors, *Bede's Ecclesiastical history of the English people* (Oxford, 1969).

Cross, F.L. and E.A. Livingstone (eds), *The Oxford dictionary of the Christian church*, 3rd ed. (Oxford, 1997).

Cunningham, B. and R. Gillespie, 'The Uí Dhomhnaill and their books in early sixteenth-century Ireland' in S. Duffy (ed.), *Princes, prelates and poets in medieval Ireland: essays in honour of Katherine Simms* (Dublin, 2013), 481–502.

Cunningham, G., *The Anglo-Norman advance into the south-west of Ireland, 1185–1221* (Roscrea, 1987).

Cunningham, G., *The round tower at Roscrea and its environs* (Roscrea, 2014).

Dalton, O.M., *The history of the Franks by Gregory of Tours*, 2 vols (Oxford, 1927).

De Smedt, C. and J. De Backer (eds), *Acta sanctorum Hiberniae ex codice Salmanticensi nunc primum integre edita* (Edinburgh and London, 1887).

Farrely, J. and C. O'Brien, *Archaeological inventory of County Tipperary*, i (N. Tipperary) (Dublin, 2002).

Flanagan, M.T., *Irish royal charters: texts and contexts* (Oxford, 2005).

Follet, W., *Céli Dé in Ireland: monastic writing and identity in the early Middle Ages* (Woodbridge, 2006).

Freeman, A.M., *The compossicion booke of Conought* (Dublin, 1936).

Gleeson, J., *History of the Ely O'Carroll territory or ancient Ormond*, 2 vols (Dublin, 1915; repr. Kilkenny, 1982).

Grosjean, P., 'Les vies de S. Columba de Tír Dá Glas' in 'Notes d'hagiographie celtique', *Analecta Bollandiana*, 72 (1954), 343–7.

Grosjean, P., 'Poems on St Senan', *Irish Texts*, 4 (1934), 68–96.

Gwynn, A. and D.F. Gleeson, *A history of the diocese of Killaloe* (Dublin, 1962).

Gwynn, A. and R.N. Hadcock, *Medieval religious houses, Ireland* (London, 1970).

Gwynn, E. (ed.), 'The rule of Tallaght', *Hermathena*, 44 (1927), i–xxvi, 1–109.

Hamann, S., 'St Fursa, the genealogy of an Irish saint: the historical person and his cult', *Proceedings of the Royal Irish Academy*, 112C (2012), 147–87.

Harbison, P., *The high crosses of Ireland*, 3 vols (Bonn, 1992).

Hayes, W.J. and J. Kennedy, *The parish churches of north Tipperary: commemorating a two-hundred-year heritage* (Roscrea, 2007).

Herbert, M., *Iona, Kells and Derry: the history and hagiography of the monastic familia of Columba* (Oxford, 1988).

Hogan, E., *Onomasticon goedelicum locorum et tribuum Hiberniae et Scotiae: an index, with identifications, to the Gaelic names of places and tribes* (Dublin and London, 1910).

Jacobsen, W., 'Saints' tombs in Frankish church architecture', *Speculum*, 72.4 (1997), 1107–43.

Jankulak, K., 'Alba longa in the Celtic regions? Swine, saints and Celtic hagiography' in J. Cartwright (ed.), *Celtic hagiography and saints' cults* (Cardiff, 2003), 271–85.

Kenney, J.F., *The sources for the early history of Ireland (ecclesiastical)* (New York, 1929; repr. Dublin, 1979).

Lewis, S., *Topographical dictionary of Ireland*, 2 vols (London, 1837).

Macalister, R.A.S. (ed.), *Book of Fenagh: supplementary volume* (Dublin, 1939).

MacCotter, P., *Medieval Ireland: territorial, political and economic divisions* (Dublin, 2008).

MacNeill, J., 'Early Irish population groups: their nomenclature, classification and chronology', *Proceedings of the Royal Irish Academy*, 29C4 (1911), 59–114.

Mac Shamhráin, A., *Church and polity in pre-Norman Ireland: the case of Glendalough* (Maynooth, 1996).

Manning, C., 'Daire Mór identified', *Peritia*, 11 (1997), 359–69.

Mc Carthy, D., 'Collation of annalistic entries referencing Roscrea' in G. Cunningham, *The round tower at Roscrea and its environs* (Roscrea, 2014), 80–1.

McInerney, L., 'A poem on the saints of Munster', *Seanchas Ard Mhacha*, 24.1 (2012), 10–22.

Meyer, K. (ed.), *The triads of Ireland* (Dublin, 1906).

Mulchrone, K. (ed.), *Bethu Phátraic. The tripartite Life of Patrick* (Dublin and London, 1939).

Ó Briain, F., 'The hagiography of Leinster' in J. Ryan (ed.), *Féilsgríbhinn Eóin Mhic Néill: essays and studies presented to Professor Eoin MacNeill* (Dublin, 1940), 454–64.

O'Brien, M.A. (ed.), *Corpus genealogiarum Hiberniae*, 1 (Dublin, 1962).

Ó Carragáin, T., *Churches in early medieval Ireland* (New Haven, CT, and London, 2010).

Ó Carragáin, T., 'Patterns of patronage: churches, round towers and the Dál Cais kings of Munster (*c.*950–1050)' in S. Brown (ed.), *Limerick and south-west Ireland: medieval art and architecture* (Leeds, 2011), 23–41.

Ó Cearbhaill, P., *Cill i logainmneacha Co. Thiobraid Árann* (Dublin, 2007).

Ó Cearbhaill, P., *Cluain i logainmneacha Co. Thiobraid Árann* (Dublin, 2010).

Ó Cíobháin, B., 'Deoisí na hÉireann i ndiaidh Sionaid Cheanannais', *Dinnseanchas*, 5 (1972), 52–6.

Ó Cíobháin, B., 'The toponomy of the peninsula of Uíbh Ráthach' in J. Crowley and J. Sheehan (eds), *The Iveragh Peninsula: a cultural atlas of the Ring of Kerry* (Cork, 2009), 81–9.

Ó Cróinín, D., *Early medieval Ireland, 400–1200* (London and New York, 1995).

O'Curry, E., *Lectures on the manuscript materials of ancient Irish history* (Dublin, 1861; repr. Dublin, 1995).

O'Daly, M., 'Mesce Chúanach', *Ériu*, 19 (1962), 75–80.

O'Flynn, E., 'The two Colmáns' in S. Duffy (ed.), *Princes, prelates and poets in medieval Ireland: essays in honour of Katherine Simms* (Dublin, 2013), 32–45.

O'Grady, S.H. (ed.), *Silva gadelica: a collection of tales in Irish*, 2 vols (London and Edinburgh, 1892).

O'Hanlon, J., *The Lives of the Irish saints*, 10 vols (Dublin, 1875–1903).

Ó hAodha, D. (ed.), *Bethu Brigte* (Dublin, 1978).

O'Keeffe, J.G., 'Cáin Domnaig', *Ériu*, 2 (1905), 189–214.

Ó Muraíle, N. (ed.), *Leabhar Mór na nGenealach: The great book of Irish genealogies, compiled by Dubhaltach Mac Fhirbhisigh*, 5 vols (Dublin, 2003).

Ó Murchadha, D., 'Early history and settlements of the Laígis' in P.G. Lane and W. Nolan (eds), *Laois, history and society* (Dublin, 2000), 35–62.

Ó Murchadha, D., *Family names of County Cork* (Dún Laoghaire, 1985).

O'Rahilly, T.F., 'The history of the Stowe Missal', *Ériu*, 10 (1926), 95–109.

Ó Riain, P., 'Another Cork charter: the Life of Saint Finbarr', *Journal of the Cork Historical and Archaeological Society*, 90 (1985), 1–13.

Ó Riain, P. (ed.), *Beatha Bharra: Saint Finbarr of Cork. The complete Life* (Dublin, 1994).

Ó Riain, P., 'Cainnech alias Colum Cille' in P. de Brún, S. Ó Coileáin and P. Ó Riain (eds), *Folia gadelica: essays presented by former students to R.A. Breatnach* (Cork, 1983), 20–35.

Ó Riain, P. (ed.), *Corpus genealogiarum sanctorum Hiberniae* (Dublin, 1985).

Ó Riain, P., *Feastdays of the saints: a history of Irish martyrologies* (Brussels, 2006).

Ó Riain, P., 'Fíonán of Iveragh' in J. Crowley and J. Sheehan (eds), *The Iveragh Peninsula: a cultural atlas of the Ring of Kerry* (Cork, 2009), 126–8.

Ó Riain, P., 'St Abbán: the genesis of an Irish saint's Life' in D.E. Evans, J.G. Griffith and E.M. Jope (eds), *Proceedings of the Seventh International Congress of Celtic Studies, Oxford, 1983* (Oxford, 1986), 159–70.

Ó Riain, P., *The making of a saint: Finbarr of Cork, 600–1200* (London, 1997).

Ó Riain, P., 'The medieval story of Saint Crónán of Roscrea' in P. Harbison and V. Hall (eds), *A carnival of learning* (Roscrea, 2012), 158–62.

Ó Riain, P., 'The O'Donohue Lives of the Salamancan Codex: the earliest collection of Irish saints' Lives?' in S. Sheehan, J. Findon and W. Follett (eds), *Gablánach in Scélaigecht: Celtic studies in honour of Ann Dooley* (Dublin, 2013), 38–52.

Ó Riain, P., 'The Psalter of Cashel: a provisional list of contents', *Éigse*, 23 (1989), 107–30.

Ó Riain, P., 'The shrine of the Stowe Missal, redated', *Proceedings of the Royal Irish Academy*, 91C10 (1991), 285–95.

Ó Riain, P., 'Towards a methodology in early Irish hagiography', *Peritia*, 1 (1982), 146–59.

Ó Riain, P., D. Ó Murchadha and K. Murray, *Historical dictionary of Gaelic place-names: Foclóir stairiúil áitainmneacha na Gaeilge*, 5 fascicles (London, 2003, 2005, 2008, 2011, 2013).

Ó Riain-Raedel, D., 'Cashel and Germany: the documentary evidence' in D. Bracken and D. Ó Riain-Raedel (eds), *Ireland and Europe in the twelfth century: reform and renewal* (Dublin, 2006), 176–217.

Pender, S., 'The O Clery book of genealogies', *Analecta Hibernica*, 18 (1951), i–xxxiii, 1–198.

Pfeil, B. (ed.), *Die Vision des Tnugdalus' Alber's von Windberg: Literatur und Frömmigkeitsgeschichte im ausgehenden 12. Jahrhundert* (Frankfurt, 1999).

Plummer, C. (ed.), *Irish litanies* (London, 1925).

Plummer, C. (ed.), *Miscellanea hagiographica Hiberniae* (Brussels, 1925).

Power, P. (ed.), *Life of St Declan of Ardmore and Life of St Mochuda of Lismore* (London, 1914).

Reeves, W. (ed.), *Ecclesiastical antiquities of Down, Connor and Dromore, consisting of a taxation of those dioceses, compiled in the year MCCVI* (Dublin, 1847).

Reeves, W. (ed.), *The Life of St Columba, founder of Hy, written by Adamnan* (Dublin and Edinburgh, 1857).

Sharpe, R., *Medieval Irish saints' Lives: an introduction to Vitae sanctorum Hiberniae* (Oxford, 1991).

Sheehy, M.P. (ed.), *Pontificia Hibernica: medieval papal chancery documents concerning Ireland, 640–1261*, 2 vols (Dublin, 1962–5).

Sperber, I., 'One saint, two fathers and three men in a boat: the Life of St Colum of Terryglass', *Celtica*, 26 (2010), 171–99.

Stokes, M. and G. Petrie, *Christian inscriptions in the Irish language* (Dublin, 1872–8).

Stokes, W. (ed.), *Lives of the saints from the Book of Lismore* (Oxford, 1890).

Stokes, W. (ed.), *The tripartite Life of St Patrick with other documents relating to that saint*, 2 vols (London, 1887).

Todd, J.H. (ed.), *Cogadh Gaedhel re Gallaibh: The war of the Gaedhil with the Gaill* (London, 1867).

Walsh, P. (ed.), *Genealogiae regum et sanctorum Hiberniae by the Four Masters*, in *Archivium Hibernicum*, 5–6 (1916–17) and separately (Maynooth and Dublin, 1918).

Walsh, P., *Irish leaders and learning through the ages*, essays collected, ed. and intr. by N. Ó Muraíle (Dublin, 2003).

Warner, G.F. (ed.), *The Stowe Missal*, 2 vols (London, 1906, 1915).

Weber, S., *Iren auf dem Kontinent: Das Leben des Marianus Scottus von Regensburg und die Anfänge der irischen 'Schottenklöster'* (Heidelberg, 2010).

White, N.B. (ed.), *Extents of Irish monastic possessions, 1540–1, from manuscripts in the Public Record Office, London* (Dublin, 1943).

Index of persons, places and peoples

Uí Mhaoile Tola 88
Uí Mheachair/Mahers 19
Uí Néill 7, 17–18, 91, 104
Uí Oilealla 71, 76, 106
Uí Shúilleabháin 96, 110
Ulster(men) 47–8, 68, 71
Upperwoods, b., LS 98

Vikings 23, 40, 66

Wales 108
Waterford, Co. 97
Westmeath, Co. xii, 1, 92, 96, 102
Wexford, friary of, WX 104

Index of subjects

alms 32, 54, 82–3
angel(s) 7, 9, 13–14, 16, 34–5, 38, 45,
    49–51, 55, 74, 77, 104, 108
annals/annalists 2, 5, 21, 23, 39–40, 68,
    87, 96, 100
aonach 23
apostles, Irish 3, 64, 86, 108
apple(s) 31, 37, 51, 92
archbishop 53, 60–1, 103

bath(ing)/wash(ing) 11, 15, 44, 50, 63,
    83, 93
beast, venemous 84, 110
beer 35–6
bee(s) 30, 34, 51
bell(s) 32, 50, 65, 75, 80, 85, 94, 99, 105
bird(s) 9, 13, 64, 88
bishops, seven 9, 86
blind 45, 63
blood, from bread 58, 83, 102
boar, wild, at site of church 50, 71, 74,
    99, 105; coffin dug out by 82
boat 14, 16, 18, 71, 78
body, dispute over 8, 17–18, 53, 62–3
Book of Díoma 27, 93
Book of Leinster 4, 14, 68, 88
book(s) 10–12, 93: gospel-book 23, 37,
    87, 96, 101; mass-book 17; book-
    chest 12
boundary 27, 51, 55, 84, 109
bread 58, 83, 102, 109
breast milk 42, 45–6
bronze 37, 77
burial practices 28, 52–3, 60, 94, 101
butter 33, 35, 84

calves 58
campus laetitiae 65
canonesses, Arroasian 6, 27, 38, 71, 79,
    108
canons, Augustinian 6, 8, 22, 26, 66–8,
    70–2, 86–7, 90, 93, 104, 107–8
canons, Premonstratensian 71, 104, 106
carnal, desire/ways 47, 56
cart(s)/wagon(s) 16, 32–3, 35, 46, 82,
    84, 98
céili Dé 4–5, 21, 23, 40, 64, 67, 94
cellarer, of church 35, 78
chains, golden 37,
charioteer, of king 80
charity 30–1
chasteness 33
chrism/chrismal 11, 53, 87
Cistercian(s) xi, 41–2, 92, 97, 103
cloak, of saint 84, 87
clothes, as payment 105
communion, last 52, 58–9, 62
corn, reaping of 56, 107
cowherds 58
cursing of Tara. *See* Tara

Day of Judgement 12, 48, 56, 60
dead, raising from 11, 14, 35, 45, 56–7,
    63, 75, 81, 83–4, 88
deaf, cured 32, 36, 82
deer 31. *See also* hind
demon(s) 25, 31, 47–8, 55–6, 72, 76,
    84–5, 110
devil 48, 79
discipline, ecclesiastical 29
dogs 15